D1321872

The **S**wallow, The **O**wl & The **S**andpiper

The Swallow, The Owl & The Sandpiper. ISBN 978-0-9563744-0-0
Published by Finks Publishing Ltd. Distributed by The Sandpiper Trust. Printed by Vision Press.
The Sandpiper Trust, The Broich, Doune, Perthshire FK16 6HJ Scottish Charity no. SCO 31165 Reg Office.
© The Sandpiper Trust
www.sandpipertrust.org

Dedicated to all those who work
in the world of pre-hospital emergency care
and in A&E departments in Scotland

And
In Memory of
Sandy Dickson
(1986-2000)

Foreword

Since it was founded in 2001, The Sandpiper Trust has made a significant difference to pre-hospital emergency care in rural Scotland and I am delighted to have played a part in its success story. It is an honour to introduce this latest work of inspiration from Claire Maitland which offers wise and thought-provoking words of wisdom contributed by Sandpiper supporters. It includes the words of encouragement spoken to the Nation by George VI in 1939 – contributed to the Sandpiper Trust by Her Majesty, The Queen.

The desire to include my words of meaning have been realised and relate to my sporting career which took me to many corners of the world and helped shape the person I am today. I always enjoyed playing my part in a team and the thinking of the coach who had the greatest influence on me, Ian McGeechan, is encapsulated in the following paragraph:

> *'Players have to have passion and emotion to succeed and achieve. Winning, and a belief in winning is emotional. It gets the adrenalin moving which sends you on a high when you win and makes you cry when you lose – because it matters. There must be passion to succeed, to achieve and to keep achieving, to raise horizons and expectations. Excellence is continuous, you've never done enough, you can never be satisfied, but as the team grows it achieves a special identity – no longer one person's image – but a reflection of everyone's interests, their abilities and their beliefs.'*

I know from experience that we all have good days and bad days. However, it is important to remember that although the path we choose to tread may appear untrodden, others have walked it before and have survived. To find the strength and motivation to get back on track when you suffer a setback may seem impossible. It takes time, courage and support. If the words of wisdom within this book help provide support to someone who is trying to get back on track, then it will have achieved its aims.

Gavin Hastings OBE – Patron of The Sandpiper Trust and former Captain of Scotland and the British Lions

The Gate of the Year
by Minnie Louise Haskins

I said to the man who stood at the gate of the year
'Give me a light that I may tread safely into the unknown.'

And he replied,
'Go into the darkness and put your hand
into the hand of God.
That shall be to you better than light and safer than a known way!'

Sent by Her Majesty, The Queen
to The Sandpiper Trust, 18th September 2008

Her father, George VI,
concluded his Christmas Day Broadcast, 1939,
with these words of encouragement.
Britain and France had declared war on Germany
just three months earlier on 3rd September 1939.
The poem had been drawn to the King's attention
by Queen Elizabeth, the present Queen's mother,
and the lines were to be recited 63 years later
at her own funeral.

Introduction

The aftermath that occurs following a sudden shock can cause a rippling effect similar to an emotional tsunami.

Tragedies do happen and we are ill-prepared for such events. Our hearts may temporarily freeze. It is only when the icicles surrounding the heart begin to thaw and the numbing sensation wears off that the pain sets in. Emotions tumble into freefall. Along with sadness may come feelings of anger, despair, confusion, isolation, fear and eventually exhaustion. We may cry when we should be laughing, and laugh when we feel like crying.

To witness the pain and anguish of a mother whose child has died, of the friend who has received the diagnosis of a terminal illness, or the parent of an anorexic child is not easy.

We all have our different mechanisms for coping. For some, they appear to brush themselves down and soldier on, for others it may not be so easy.
For them, it may be the beginning of an uphill struggle, a journey which takes courage, wisdom, spirit and sometimes hardest of all, patience. It is my hope that the words in this book The Swallow, The Owl and The Sandpiper contributed from Sandpiper Trust supporters, will provide strength and comfort not only to those venturing out on this journey but also to their friends and family who are so important in providing support.

This anthology starts with the Courage of the intrepid Swallow, who journeys thousands of miles annually in order to raise its young, overcoming endless challenges and hurdles along the way, brief encounters, highs and lows, twists and turns.
It also has the Wisdom of the Owl who watches quietly, who listens patiently, who learns, and who leads by example and experience.
It concludes with the Spirit of the little Sandpiper, forging lifelong friendships, rainy days and sunshine, tears, smiles and memories…

Claire Maitland – *The Sandpiper Trust*

The Swallow

for courage

• •

'Do you know,' Peter asked,
'why swallows build in the eaves of houses?
It is to listen to the stories.'
Peter Pan

Don't Quit *by Jill Wolf*

Don't quit when the tide is lowest,
For its just about to turn,
Don't quit over doubts and questions,
For there's something you may learn.
Don't quit when the night is darkest,
For its just a while 'til dawn;
Don't quit when you've run the farthest,
For the race is almost won.
Don't quit when the hill is steepest,
For your goal is almost nigh;
Don't quit for you're not a failure
Until you fail to try.

• • •

As you journey through life,
  choose your destinations well but do not hurry there.
You will arrive soon enough.
Wander the back roads and forgotten paths,
  keeping your destination in your heart,
  like a fixed point of a compass.
Seek out new voices, strange sights,
  and ideas foreign to your own.
Such things are riches for the soul.
And if, upon arrival you find that your destination
  is not exactly as you dreamed,
  do not be disappointed.
Think of all you would have missed but for the journey there,
  and know that the true worth of your travels lies
  not in the journey's end,
  but in whom you come to be along the way. *anon.*

• • •

The Road Not Taken *by Robert Frost (1874-1963)*

Two roads diverged in a yellow wood
and sorry I could not travel both
And be one traveller, long I stood
and looked down one as far as I could
to where it bent in the undergrowth;

> Then took the other, as just as fair,
> and having perhaps the better claim
> because it was grassy and wanted wear;
> though as for that, the passing there
> had worn them really about the same,

And both that morning equally lay
in leaves no feet had trodden black.
Oh, I kept the first for another day!
Yet knowing how way leads on to way,
I doubted if I should ever come back.

> I shall be telling this with a sigh
> Somewhere ages and ages hence:
> Two roads diverged in a wood, and I –
> I took the one less travelled by,
> and that has made all the difference.

• • •

I never saw a wild thing
Sorry for itself.
A small bird will drop frozen dead from a bough
Without ever having felt sorry for itself.

D.H.Lawrence (1885-1930)

Rose Beyond the Wall *by A.L. Frink*

A rose once grew
where all could see,
sheltered beside
a garden wall,
And as the days passed
swiftly by,
it spread its branches, straight and tall...

One day, a beam of light
shone through
a crevice that had
opened wide ~
The rose bent gently
toward its warmth
then passed beyond
to the other side.

Now, you who deeply
feel its loss,
be comforted ~ the rose blooms there ~
its beauty even greater now,
nurtured by
God's own loving care.

• • •

Dear God, be good to me;
The sea is so wide,
And my boat is so small.

Breton Fisherman's Prayer

The Fifth Mountain *by Paolo Coelho*

A warrior accepts defeat. He does not treat it as a matter of indifference, nor does he attempt to transform it into a victory. The pain of defeat is bitter to him; he suffers at indifference and becomes desperate with loneliness. After all this has passed, he licks his wounds and begins everything anew. A warrior knows that war is made of many battles; he goes on. Tragedies do happen.

We can discover the reason, blame others, imagine how different our lives would be had they not occurred. But none of that is important: they did occur, and so be it.

From there onward we must put aside the fear that they awoke in us and begin to rebuild.

• • •

A Scottish Gaelic Prayer

As the rain hides the stars,
as the autumn mist hides the hills,
as the clouds veil the blue of the sky,
so the dark happenings of my lot hide the shining of thy face from me.

Yet, if I may hold thy hand in the darkness,
it is enough, since I know,
that though I may stumble in my going,
You do not fall. *anon.*

• • •

Everything passes and vanishes;
Everything leaves its trace:
And often you see in a footstep
What you could not see in a face
William Allingham   1824 - 1889

Forever Young *by Bob Dylan*

May God bless and keep you always
May your wishes all come true,
May you always do for others
And let others do for you.
May you build a ladder to the stars
And climb on every rung,
May you stay forever young,
Forever young, forever young,
May you stay forever young.

May you grow up to be righteous,
May you grow up to be true,
May you always know the truth
And see the lights surrounding you.
May you always be courageous,
Stand upright and be strong,
May you stay forever young,
Forever young, forever young,
May you stay forever young.

May your hands always be busy,
May your feet always be swift,
May you have a strong foundation
When the winds of changes shift.
May your heart always be joyful,
May your song always be sung,
May you stay forever young,
Forever young, forever young,
May you stay forever young.

• • •

Every Second Counts

•••

Grief is a tidal wave that overtakes you,
smashes down upon you with unimaginable force,
sweeps you up into its darkness,
where you tumble and crash against unidentifiable surfaces,
only to be thrown out on an unknown beach, bruised,
reshaped...
Grief will make a new person out of you,
if it doesn't kill you in the making.

Stephanie Ericsson

The Wreck on Highway 109 *by Ruth Gillis*

A drunk man in an Oldsmobile
they said had run the light
that caused the six-car pileup
on 109 that night.
When broken bodies lay about
and blood was everywhere,
the sirens screamed out elegies,
for death was in the air.

**A mother, trapped inside her car,
was heard above the noise;
her plaintive plea near split the air:
"Oh, God, please spare my boys!"
She fought to loose her pinioned hands;
she struggled to get free,
but mangled metal held her fast
in grim captivity.**

Her frightened eyes then focused on
where the back seat once had been,
but all she saw was broken glass
and two children's seats crushed in.
Her twins were nowhere to be seen;
she did not hear them cry,
and then she prayed they'd been thrown free,
"Oh, God, don't let them die!"

**Then firemen came and cut her loose,
but when they searched the back,
they found therein no little boys,
but the seat belts were intact.
They thought the woman had gone mad
and was travelling alone,
but when they turned to question her,
they discovered she was gone.**

Policemen saw her running wild
and screaming above the noise
in beseeching supplication,
"Please help me find my boys!
They're four years old and wear blue shirts;
their jeans are blue to match."
One cop spoke up, "They're in my car,
and they don't have a scratch.

They said their daddy put them there
and gave them each a cone,
then told them both to wait for Mum
to come and take them home.
I've searched the area high and low,
but I can't find their dad.
He must have fled the scene, I guess,
and that is very bad."

The mother hugged the twins and said,
while wiping at a tear,
"He could not flee the scene, you see,
for he's been dead a year."
The cop just looked confused and asked,
"Now, how can that be true?"
The boys said, "Mummy, Daddy came
and left a kiss for you.

He told us not to worry
and that you would be all right,
and then he put us in this car
with the pretty, flashing light.
We wanted him to stay with us,
because we miss him so,
but Mummy, he just hugged us tight
and said he had to go.

The Swallow

He said someday we'd understand
and told us not to fuss,
and he said to tell you, Mummy,
he's watching over us."
The mother knew without a doubt
that what they spoke was true,
for she recalled their dad's last words,
"I will watch over you."

**The firemen's notes could not explain
the twisted, mangled car,
and how the three of them escaped
without a single scar.
But on the cop's report was scribed,
in print so very fine,
'An angel walked the beat tonight'.**

• • •

*Ever tried? Ever failed?
No matter.
Try again. Fail again.
Fail better.*   *Samuel Beckett (1906-1989)*

Face the days that lie ahead with a spirit of adventure, compassion, honesty and confidence. Brave the stormy seas that are bound to confront you, determined to sail your ship on to the quiet waters that lie ahead. Help those whom you may find in trouble and steer clear of the whirlpool of destruction which you will meet on your voyage through life. Be not afraid of who you are, what you are or where you are, but cling implicitly to the Truth as taught in the religion of your following. If you do all these things, you will be 'of service'. If you are 'of service' you will make others happy and you will be happy too.

written for Kurt Hahn
Founder of Gordonstoun School *by Sir Iain Tennant*

• • •

When things go wrong, as they sometimes will,
When the road you're trudging seems all uphill,
When the funds are low and the debts are high,
And you want to smile, but you have to sigh,
When care is pressing you down a bit-
Rest if you must, but don't you quit.
Life is strange with its twists and turns,
As every one of us sometimes learns,
And many a fellow turns about
When he might have won had he stuck it out.
Don't give up though the pace seems slow -
You may succeed with another blow.
Success is failure turned inside out -
The silver tint in the clouds of doubt,
And you never can tell how close you are,
It might be near when it seems afar;
So stick to the fight when you're hardest hit -
It's when things seem worst that you must not quit.
anon.

The Swallow

'I Am There'

by Iris Hesselden (amended)

Look for me when the tide is high
And the swallows are wheeling overhead
When the autumn wind sweeps the cloudy sky
And one by one the leaves are shed
Look for me when the trees are bare
And the stars are bright in the frosty sky
When the morning mist hangs on the air
And shorter darker days pass by.

I am there, where the river flows
And salmon leap to a silver moon
Where the insects hum and the tall grass grows
And sunlight warms the afternoon
I am there in the busy street
I take you hand in the city square
In the market place where the people meet
In your quiet room – I am there

I am the love you cannot see
And all I ask is – look for me.

• • •

A bright flame before me,
A guiding star above me,
A smooth path beneath me,
A kindly shepherd behind me.

• • •

If you think you are beaten – you are!
    If you think you dare not – you don't
If you'd like to win, but think you can't
    It's almost a cinch you won't.
If you think you'll lose, you've lost,
    For out in the world we find,
Success begins with a fellow's will,
    It's all in the state of mind.
Life's battles don't always go
    To the stronger or faster man,
But sooner or later the man who wins,
    Is the man who thinks he can!

by Walter D Wintle

• • •

Another and another and another *by James Henry*

Another and another and another
And still another sunset and sunrise,
The same yet different, different yet the same,
Seen by me now in my declining years
As in my early childhood, youth and manhood;
And by my parents and my parents' parents,
And by the parents of my parents' parents
And by their parents counted back for ever,
Seen, all their lives long, even as now by me;
And by my children and my children's children
And by the children of my children's children
And by their children counted on for ever
Still to be seen as even now seen by me;
Clear and bright sometimes, sometimes dark and clouded
But still the same sunsetting and sunrise;
The same for ever to the never ending
Line of observers, to the same observer
Through all the changes of his life the same:
Sunsetting and sunrising and sunsetting,
Sunrising and sunsetting evermore

Our Quilt of Life

As I faced my Maker at the last judgment, I knelt before the Lord along with all the other souls. Before each of us laid our lives like the squares of a quilt in many piles.

An Angel sat before each of us sewing our quilt squares together into a tapestry that is our life. But as my angel took each piece of cloth off the pile, I noticed how ragged and empty each of my squares was. They were filled with giant holes. Each square was labelled with a part of my life that had been difficult, the challenges and temptations I was faced with in everyday life. I saw hardships that I endured, which were the largest holes of all.

I glanced around me. Nobody else had such squares. Other than a tiny hole here and there, the other tapestries were filled with rich colour and the bright hues of worldly fortune.

I gazed upon my own life and was disheartened. My angel was sewing the ragged pieces of cloth together, threadbare and empty, like binding air.

Finally, the time came when each life was to be displayed, held up to the light, the scrutiny of truth. The others rose, each in turn, holding up their tapestries. So filled their lives had been.

My angel looked upon me, and nodded for me to rise. My gaze dropped to the ground in shame. I hadn't had all the earthly fortunes. I had love in my life, and laughter. But there had also been trials of illness, and death, and false accusations that took from me my world as I knew it. I had to start over many times.

I often struggled with the temptation to quit, only to somehow muster the strength to pick up and begin again. I spent many nights on my knees in prayer, asking for help and guidance in my life. I had often been held up to ridicule, which I endured painfully, each time offering it up to the Father in hopes that I would not melt within my skin beneath the judgmental gaze of those who unfairly judged me.

And now, I had to face the truth. My life was what it was, and I had to accept it for what it was. I rose and slowly lifted the combined squares of my life to the light. An awe-filled gasp filled the air. I gazed around at the others who stared at me with wide eyes.

Then, I looked upon the tapestry before me. Light flooded the many holes, creating an image, the face of Christ. Then our Lord stood before me, with warmth and love in His eyes. He said, every time you gave over your life to Me, it became My life, My hardships, and My struggles. Each point of light in your life is when you stepped aside and let Me shine through, until there was more of Me than there was of you. May all our quilts be threadbare and worn, allowing Christ to shine through. May God Bless You This Day. *anon.*

•••

Positive Count

Count your blessings instead of your crosses,
Count your gains instead of your losses,
Count your joys instead of your woes,
Count your friends instead of your foes,
Count your courage instead of your fears,
Count your laughs instead of your tears,
Count your full years instead of your lean,
Count your kind deeds instead of your mean,
Count your health instead of your wealth,
Count on your God instead of yourself. *anon.*

•••

''Far better is it to dare mighty things even though chequered by failure than to dwell in that perpetual twilight that knows not victory or defeat.'' Theodore Roosevelt

We Remember Them

At the rising of the sun and its going down,
we remember them.

> At the blowing of the wind and in the chill of winter,
> **we remember them.**

At the opening of the buds and in the rebirth of spring,
we remember them.

> At the blueness of the skies and in the warmth of summer,
> **we remember them.**

At the rustling of the leaves and in the beauty of autumn,
we remember them.

> At the beginning of the year and when it ends,
> **we remember them.**

As long as we live, they too will live;
for they are now a part of us, as **we remember them.**

> When we are weary and in need of strength,
> **we remember them.**

When we are lost and sick at heart,
we remember them.

> When we have joy we crave to share,
> **we remember them.**

When we have decisions that are difficult to make,
we remember them.

> When we have achievements that are based on theirs,
> **we remember them.**

As long as we live, they, too, will live;
for they are now a part of us, as **we remember them.** *anon..*

Deep within me
there are resources
to meet every crisis
I shall encounter.
I live every day
as best I can, in the
sure and certain grace
that power
is built into me,
to handle everything
that shall ever come
to me. *anon.*

•••

The Swallow

A Song of Living *by Amelia Josephine Burr (1878-1968)*

Because I have loved life, I shall have no sorrow to die.
I have sent up my gladness on wings, to be lost in the blue of the sky.
I have run and leaped with the rain, I have taken the wind to my breast.
My cheek like a drowsy child to the face of the earth I have pressed.
Because I have loved life, I shall have no sorrow to die.

I have kissed young Love on the lips, I have heard his song to the end,
I have struck my hand like a seal in the loyal hand of a friend.
I have known the peace of heaven, the comfort of work done well.
I have longed for death in the darkness and risen alive out of hell.
Because I have loved life, I shall have no sorrow to die.

I give a share of my soul to the world where my course is run.
I know that another shall finish the task I must leave undone.
I know that no flower, nor flint was in vain on the path I trod.
As one looks on a face through a window, through life
I have looked on God,
Because I have loved life, I shall have no sorrow to die.

• • •

From the Sound of Music *by Rodgers and Hammerstein*

Climb every mountain, search high and low
Follow every byway, every path you know.
Climb every mountain, ford every stream,
Follow every rainbow, 'til you find your dream!

A dream that will need
all the love you can give,
Every day of your life
for as long as you live.

Climb every mountain, ford every stream,
Follow every rainbow, 'til you find your dream!

Birth is a beginning
And death a destination.
And life is a journey:
From childhood to maturity
And youth to age;
From innocence to awareness
And ignorance to knowing:
From foolishness to discretion
And then, perhaps to wisdom;
From weakness to strength
Or strength to weakness-
And, often, back again;
From health to sickness
And back, we pray, to health again;
From offense to forgiveness
From loneliness to love,
From joy to gratitude,
From pain to compassion,
From fear to faith;
From defeat to defeat to defeat-
Until, looking backward or ahead,
We see that victory lies
Not at some high place along the way,
But in having made the journey, stage by stage,
A sacred pilgrimage.
Birth is a beginning
And death is a destination.
And life is a journey,
A sacred pilgrimage -
To life everlasting. *anon.*

The Return
Found in the prayer book of Wilfred, 3rd Baron, Lord Glanusk

The stag's on the hilltop, the grouse on the wing

All the glories of Scotland, so lovely a thing.

I behold them again, through the mist in my eyes.

While they seem immortal, the human frame dies.

The curlew is calling, as old to his mate.

The brown trout are jumping, the burn is in spate.

The lights and the shadow, steal over the heather.

These things we have loved, and shared both together.

The rollers are breaking, below on the shore.

Oh surely somewhere, you will see them once more.

All the wonder of mountains, the blue of the sea.

Yet you'll never come back, to share them with me.

• • •

*'I was taught that the way of
progress is neither swift nor easy.'*

Marie Curie (1867 - 1934)

CARPE DIEM

seize the day

Cancer is so limited...

It cannot cripple love.
It cannot shatter hope.
It cannot corrode faith.
It cannot eat away peace.
It cannot destroy confidence.
It cannot kill friendship.
It cannot cut out memories.
It cannot silence courage.
It cannot invade the soul.
It cannot reduce eternal life.
It cannot quench the spirit.
It cannot lessen the power of the Resurrection.
anon.

• • •

Do not let your hearts be troubled. Trust in God; Trust also in me. In my Father's house are many rooms; if it were not so, I would have told you. I am going there to prepare a place for you. And if I go and prepare a place for you, I will come back and take you to be with me that you also may be where I am. *John 14:1-3*

• • •

Tightrope *from Kingfisher Days by Mary Sheepshanks*

Do not look down
But keep eyes trained
upon a pinpoint star
of flickering hope,
To edge a way
across this frayed,
Precarious bridge of mystery.

Is there a safety net should I slip?

Clouds

Down the blue night the unending columns press
In noiseless tumult, break and wave and flow,
Now tread the far South, or lift rounds of snow
Up the white moon's hidden loveliness.

Some pause in their grave wandering comradeless,
And turn with profound gesture vague and slow,
As who would pray good for the world, but know
Their benediction empty as they bless.

They say that the Dead die not, but remain
Near to the rich heirs of their grief and mirth.

I think they ride the calm mid-heaven, as these,
In wise majestic melancholy train,
And watch the moon, and the still-raging seas,
And men, coming and going on the earth.

Rupert Brooke, written in October 1913 somewhere in the Pacific

• ● •

I like living.
I have sometimes been wildly,
despairingly, acutely miserable,
racked with sorrow,
but through it all I still know
that just to be alive is a grand thing.

Agatha Christie

The Swallow

Thich Nhat Hanh *from Earth Prayers*

Do not say that I'll depart tomorrow because even today I still arrive.

Look deeply: I arrive in every second to be a bud on a spring branch,
to be a tiny bird, with wings still fragile, learning to sing in my new nest,
to be a caterpillar in the heart of a flower, to be a jewel hiding itself
in a stone.

I still arrive, in order to laugh and to cry, in order to fear and to hope,
the rhythm of my heart is the birth and death of all that are alive.

I am the mayfly metamorphosing in the surface of the river,
and I am the bird which, when spring comes, arrives in time
to eat the mayfly.

I am the frog swimming happily in the clear water of a pond,
and I am also the grass-snake who, approaching in silence,
feeds itself on the frog.

I am the child in Uganda, all skin and bones, my legs as thin as bamboo
sticks, and I am the arms merchant, selling deadly weapons to Uganda.

I am the 12-year-old girl, refugee on a small boat,
who throws herself into the ocean after being raped by a sea pirate,
and I am the pirate, my heart not yet capable of seeing and loving.

I am a member of the politburo, with plenty of power in my hand,
and I am the man who has to pay his 'debt of blood' to my people,
dying slowly in a forced labour camp.

My joy is like spring, so warm it makes flowers bloom in all walks of life.

My pain is like a river of tears, so full it fills up the four oceans.

Please call me by my true names, so I can hear all my cries and my laughs
at once, so I can see that my joy and pain are one.

Please call me by my true names, so I can wake up,
and so the door of my heart can be left open, the door of compassion.

Fisherman's Prayer

God grant that I may live to fish
until my dying day.
And when it comes to my last cast,
I then most humble pray,
When in the Lord's safe
landing net
I'm peacefully asleep,
that in His mercy I be judged
as big enough to keep.

• • •

The Ship *by Bishop Blunt*

I am standing on the sea shore.
A ship sails to the morning breeze and starts for the ocean.
She is an object of beauty and I stand watching her till
at last she fades on the horizon,
and someone at my side says, 'She is gone'.

Gone where?
Gone from my sight, that is all;
she is just as large in the masts, hull and spars as she ever was
when I saw her,
and just as able to bear her load to her destination.

The diminished size and total loss of sight is in me, not in her;
and just at the moment when someone at my side says,
"She is gone",
there are others who are watching her coming,
and other voices take up the glad shout,
'There she comes'.
And that is dying.

• • •

The Swallow

The Dragonfly *by Doris Stickney*

Once, in a little pond, in the muddy water under the lily pads,
there lived a little water beetle in a community of water beetles.
They lived a simple and comfortable life in the pond
with few disturbances and interruptions.

Once in a while, sadness would come to the community
when one of their fellow beetles would climb the stem of a lily pad
and would never be seen again. They knew when this happened
their friend was dead, gone forever.

Then, one day, one little water beetle felt an irresistible urge to climb up
that stem. However, he was determined that he would not leave forever.
He would come back and tell his friends what he had found at the top.
When he reached the top and climbed out of the water onto the surface
of the lily pad, he was so tired, and the sun felt so warm, that he decided
he must take a nap.

As he slept, his body changed and when he woke up, he had turned
into a beautiful blue-tailed dragonfly with broad wings and a slender
body designed for flying. So, fly he did! And, as he soared he saw
the beauty of a whole new world and a far superior way of life to
what he had never known existed.

Then he remembered his beetle friends and how they were thinking by
now he was dead. He wanted to go back to tell them, and explain to them
that he was now more alive than he had ever been before.
His life had been fulfilled rather than ended.
But, his new body would not go down into the water.
He could not get back to tell his friends the good news.
Then he understood that their time would come,
when they, too, would know what he now knew.
So, he raised his wings and flew off into his joyous new life!

* Doris Stickney and her minister husband
were looking for a meaningful way to explain to
neighborhood children the death of a five year old
friend. They needed an explanation that would
satisfy not only the children but adults too. While
they were preparing for the child's memorial
service the fable of the water bug that changed
into a dragonfly came to mind. "Water Bugs and
Dragonflies" tells the story of a small colony of
water bugs living happily below the surface of a
quiet pond. Every so often one of them climbs up a
lily stalk and disappears from sight, never to return.
Those left behind are faced with the mystery of
figuring out what has become of them, revealing the
"miracle that makes shiny dragonflies out of ugly
bugs", this graceful story reminds us that God has
given us the means of transforming our metaphorical
selves into dragonflies capable of winging off
contentedly into a new world. Recognising that
"the old answers will not satisfy today's children",
Doris Stickney presents instead a simple, wise
tale that illuminates a difficult reality without
pretending to contain all the answers.

•••

'Courage
is not the lack of fear,
it is the mastering of it'

Words from a mother following the loss of her son.

The Swallow

**Anonymous words written about
a Colonel in the American Civil War**

He asked for strength that he might achieve:
he was made weak that he might obey.

He asked for health that he might do greater things:
he was given infirmity that he might do better things.

He asked for riches that he might be happy:
he was given poverty that he might be wise.

He asked for power that he might have the praise of men:
he was given weakness that he might feel the need of God.

He asked for all things that he might enjoy life:
he was given life that he might enjoy all things.

He has received nothing that he asked for, all things that he hoped for.
His prayer is answered. He is most blest.

• • •

**Fair Jesus, you guide your straying sheep along lush
and fragrant valleys, where the grass is rich and deep.**

**You guard them from the attacks of wolves,
and from the bites of snakes.**

**You heal their diseases, and teach them always to walk
in the ways of God.**

**When we stray, lead us back; when temptation besets us,
give us strength; when our souls are sick, pour upon us your love.**

• • •

Speak to me by *Chief Dan George, (1899–1981)*

The beauty of the trees,
the softness of the air,
the fragrance of the grass,
speaks to me.

The summit of the mountain,
the thunder of the sky,
the rhythm of the sea,
speaks to me.

The faintness of the stars,
the freshness of the morning,
the dew drop on the flower,
speaks to me.

The strength of fire,
the taste of salmon,
the trail of the sun,
and the life that never goes away,
They speak to me.

And my heart soars.

• • •

*There are some things
you learn best in calm,
and some in storm.*

The Platform Ticket – memories and musings of a hospice doctor
by Dr. Derek Doyle (palliative care specialist)

I asked her how I could help her and her answer took me by surprise.

'A bit of me is excited, in fact very excited, just as you feel when you have seen a holiday place advertised in one of those glossy brochures but never been there and more to the point, never met anyone who has. It is a curious feeling when you only have a single and not a return ticket because you know for a certainty that you are not coming back. I have had my bag packed for a very long time. It's a bit like British Rail. You know the train will come but when is another matter altogether!
Believe me, waiting on this platform is a very lonely experience. Until that train comes in... well, I would love you to stand beside me. For that you will need to purchase a platform ticket!

When I was young they only allowed you to go on a platform if you had a ticket for the train or if you had a platform ticket for your loved one or friend. They only cost a penny, but what joy it was to stand together a little longer at such little cost. I suspect we all like someone with us when we go off on a long journey, don't you think?'

Each day I went to see her and she just shook her head and told me I was not needed. Days went by and then one day, she whispered 'Have you got your ticket?' I reassured her that I carried it with me wherever I went. She invited me to come in and sit beside her, which I did.

'Oh what a curious feeling to be so lonely and at the same time so excited,' she explained. 'We don't need to talk, you know, but I need to know that as the train comes in you'll stay beside me until I tell you. That's the point when I shall have to leave go of your hand and take the last step on my own. I know I will manage if you are near me. Sometimes we need doctors and sometimes we need friends. It is best of all when our doctors are also our friends. Thank you, dear, for being my friend. You cannot come any further but don't worry, I can manage now. She smiled as she loosened her grip on my hand.

It is difficult to describe atmosphere and ambience. Sitting with this lady was to experience a peace that is so rare in life. I think other doctors would agree with me that we are trained to talk but not how to remain silent. We are taught how to explain but not how to listen. We are taught how to be energetic but never how to restore peace and tranquility by our inactivity. We are taught nothing of inner peace, nor of loneliness and nothing whatsoever of the power of love and undemanding companionship. Those minutes which followed were some of life's richest for me.

What an honour it was to be asked to get that platform ticket and to sit with her and wait for her train to come in, all packed and ready to go.

• ● •

I will not live an unlived life *by Dawna Markova*

I will not live an unlived life
I will not live in fear of falling
Or of catching fire
I choose to inhabit my days
To allow my living to open me
Making me less afraid
More accessible
To loosen my heart
So that it becomes a wing, a torch, a promise
I choose to risk my significance.
To live so that that which comes to me as seed
Goes to the next as blossom
And that which comes to me as blossom
Goes on as fruit.

• ● •

The Velveteen Rabbit *by Margery Williams (1881-1944)*

'How can I become real?' the little velveteen rabbit asked
the old rocking horse.

'It's something that happens to you when someone loves you, for a long
time, really loves you.'

'Does it hurt?'

'Sometimes,' answered the rocking horse, 'but when you are real you don't
mind being hurt. It doesn't happen all at once, you slowly become it.
It takes a long time, and it does not often happen to people who break
easily, or have sharp edges.
'By the time you are real your velvet will be worn out and loved off, and
you will look really shabby, but these things don't matter at all because
once you are real you can't be ugly, except to people who don't know
how to love.'

•••

What if you slept?
And what if in your sleep, you dreamed?
And what if in your dream,
you went to heaven and there plucked a
strange and beautiful flower?
And what if, when you woke,
you had the flower in your hand?
Ah! What then?

Samuel Taylor Coleridge (1772-1834)

Farewell my friends.
It was beautiful as long as it lasted
The journey of my life.
I have no regrets whatsoever
Save the pain I'll leave behind.
Those dear hearts who love and care
And the heavy with sleep, ever-moist eyes.
The smile in spite of a lump in the throat
And the strings pulling at the heart and soul.
The strong arms that held me up
When my own strength let me down.
Each morsel that I was fed
Was full of love.
At every turning of my life I came across good friends,
Friends who stood by me
Even when the time raced me by.
Farewell, farewell my friends,
I smile and bid you goodbye.
No, shed no tears for I need them not,
All I need is your smile.
If you feel sad, do think of me
For that is what I'll like,
When you live in the hearts of those you love
Remember then
You never die.

Rabindranath Tagore (1861-1941)
Nobel Prize for Literature 1913

The Swallow

Happy the Man *by John Dryden (1631-1700)*

Happy the man, and happy he alone,
He who can call today his own:
He who, secure within, can say,
Tomorrow do thy worst, for I have lived today.

Be fair or foul or rain or shine
The joys I have possessed, in spite of fate, are mine.
Not Heaven itself upon the past has power,
But what has been, has been, and I have had my hour.

• • •

My Hands *by Lindsay MB*

I held a newborn boy as he took his first breath;
I felt joy.

I held an old woman's hand as she told me of her pain;
I felt compassion.

I held a young man's head with a broken neck;
I felt fortunate.

I held my breath while intubating a man whose body held too many drugs;
I felt incensed.

I held a child's lifeless heart, shattered by violence;
I felt powerless.

Driving home, I passed a homeless man who held out his hand for charity;
I felt dispirited.

I held my infant daughter while she slept;
I felt love.

I thank God for my hands.

Seaside Golf *by John Betjeman (1906-1984)*

How straight it flew, how long it flew,
It clear'd the rutty track
And soaring, disappeared from view
Beyond the bunker's back –
A glorious, sailing, bounding drive
That made me glad I was alive.

And down the fairway, far along
It glowed a lonely white;
I played an iron sure and strong
And clipped it out of sight,
And spite of grassy banks between
I knew I'd find it on the green.

And so I did. It lay content
Two paces from the pin;
A steady putt and then it went
Oh, most securely in.
The very turf rejoiced to see
That quite unprecedented three.

Ah! Seaweed smells from sandy caves
And thyme and mist in whiffs,
In-coming tide, Atlantic waves
Slapping the sunny cliffs,
Lark song and sea sounds in the air
And splendour, splendour everywhere.

• • •

No emergency is so urgent as to justify an accident

Brian Carlin – BASICS-Scotland

The Swallow

Caledonia *by Dougie MacLean*

I don't know if you can see, the changes that have come over me
In these last few days I've been afraid, that I might drift away.
So I've been telling old stories, singing songs, that make me think about
where I came from.
That's the reason why I seem so far away today.

Let me tell you that I love you, that I think about you all the time.
Caledonia, you're calling me, now I'm going home.
But if I should become a stranger, you know that it would make me
more than sad,
Caledonia's been everything I've ever had.

Now I have moved and I've kept on moving, proved the points
that I needed proving,
Lost the friends that I needed losing, found others on the way.
I have kissed the ladies and left them crying, stolen dreams,
yes there's no denying.
I have travelled hard with conscience flying, somewhere in the wind.

Now I'm sitting here before the fire, the empty room, the forest choir.
The flames have cooled, don't get any higher, they've withered
now they've gone.
But I'm steady thinking my way is clear, and I know what
I will do tomorrow,
When the hands are shaken, the kisses flow, then I will disappear.

• • •

I expect to pass through this world but once.
Any good, therefore, that I can do or any
kindness I can show to any fellow creature, let
me do it now. Let me not defer or neglect it for
I shall not pass this way again. *Stephen Grellet (1773-1855)*

I felt as if I were walking with destiny, and that all my past life has been but a preparation for this hour and this trial. Winston Churchill

• • •

I will go with my Father a-ploughing *by Joseph Campbell*

I will go with my Father a-ploughing
To the Green Field by the sea,
And the rooks and crows and seagulls
Will come flocking after me,
I will sing to the patient horses
With the lark in the shine of the air,
And my Father will sing the Plough-Song
That blesses the cleaving share.

I will go with my Father a-sowing
To the Red Field by the sea,
And blackbirds and robins and thrushes
Will come flocking after me.
I will sing to the striding sowers
With the finch on the flowering sloe,
And my Father will sing the Seed-Song
That only the wise men know.

I will go with my Father a-reaping
To the Brown Field by the sea,
And the geese and pigeons and sparrows
Will come flocking after me.
I will sing to the weary reapers
With the wren in the heat of the sun,
And my Father will sing the Scythe-Song
That joys for the harvest done.

The Swallow

I see myself now at the end of my journey, my toilsome days are ended. I am going now to see that head that was crowned with thorns, and that face that was spit upon for me. I have formerly lived by hearsay and faith but now I go where I shall live by sight, and shall be with him in whose company I delight myself. I have loved to hear my Lord spoken of; and wherever I have seen the print of this shoe in the earth, there I have coveted to set my foot to. His name to me has been as a civet-box; yea, sweeter than all perfume. His voice to me has been most sweet; and his countenance I have more desired than they that have most desired the light of the sun. His word I did use to gather for my food, and for antidotes against my faintings. 'He has held me, and hath kept me from mine iniquities; yea, my steps hath he strengthened in his way.' Glorious it was to see how the open region was filled with horses and chariots, with trumpeters and pipers, with singers and players on stringed instruments, to welcome the Pilgrims as they went up, and followed one another in at the beautiful gate of the city.

• • •

'God gave us memories so we could have roses in December'

• • •

The Swallows *by Andrew Young*

The swallows twisting here and there
Round unseen corners of the air
Upstream and down so quickly passed
I wondered that their shadows flew as fast

• • •

Winds of Fate *by Ella Wheeler Wilcox*

One ship drives east and another drives west
With the selfsame winds that blow.
'Tis the set of the sails
And not the gales
Which tells us the way to go.
Like the winds of the sea are the ways of fate,
As we voyage along through life:
'Tis the set of the soul
That decides its goal,
And not the calm or the strife.

• ● •

Autumn Rain *by Mary Frye 1932*

In those quiet moments in the still of the night
Remember to rejoice and celebrate life
Do not think of me gone and weep
I am not there, I do not sleep
I am a thousand winds that blow
I am the diamond glints on snow
I am the sunlight on the grain
I am the gentle autumn's rain
When you awaken in the morning hush
I am the swift uplifting rush
of quiet birds in flight
I am the soft stars that shine
You will hear my gentle voice
and remember to rejoice
Never give up your fight
and remember always
to Celebrate Life...

• ● •

I May Never See Tomorrow

I may never see tomorrow;
there's no written guarantee
and things that happened yesterday
belong to history.
I cannot predict the future,
I cannot change the past,
I have just the present moments,
I must treat it as my last.

I must use this moment wisely
for it soon will pass away,
and be lost forever,
as part of yesterday.
I must exercise compassion,
help the fallen to their feet,
Be a friend unto the friendless,
make an empty life complete.

The unkind things that I do today
may never be undone,
and friendships that I fail to win
may nevermore be won.
I may not have another chance
on bended knees to pray,
to thank God with a humble heart
for giving me this day. *anon*.

•••

*No-one ever told me
that grief felt so like fear*

C.S Lewis (1898-1963) *from A Grief Observed*

Gongorine sonnet
in which the poet sends his loved one a pigeon
by Federico Garcia Lorca

I send to you this Turian dove,
with sweet eyes and white plumage,
which spills, above the Grecian laurels,
a slow flame of love.

Its purity, its tender neck,
in double linen of warm froth,
trembling of frost, and pearl, and mist,
denotes the absence of your lips.

Pass your hand across this dove
and you will see its snowy melody
scatter in flakes above your beauty.

Thus my heart by night and day,
sealed in the prison of dark love,
weeps and grieves while you're away.

• • •

Heaven Haven (a nun takes the veil)
by Gerard Manley Hopkins (1844-1889)

I have desired to go
Where springs not fail,
To fields where flies no sharp and sided hail
And a few lilies blow.

And I have asked to be
Where no storms come,
Where the green swell is in the havens dumb,
And out of the swing of the sea.

The Swallow

Senses *by Dr Shona Armstrong*

Love and loyalty drowned in an instant
A revelation to shock
Devotion and friendship destroyed
Betrayal and deceit cloud emotion to numbness and disbelief
The broken mind wrestles with self doubt and shattered confidence
Torture and anguish of fragmented sleep
The pain of living dulls the senses to emptiness and loneliness
Dark, foreboding thoughts of despair and self destruction
And yet, there is a glimmer of hope
A brush with nature's healing powers brings comfort
The gushing burn
Swish of wind through the trees
Vibrant green of Blaeberry bush
Vivid yellow of gorse and broom
Scent of wet pine and heather bloom
Peaty chill of spring water
Bitter taste of juniper berry
Crunch of crisp, corrie snow
Soft, gentle sponge of moss underfoot
Birdsong rhythm of the forest canopy
Graceful flight of the soaring eagle
Dippers flitting on the rocky river
Gentle plop of the salmon leaping
Busy antics of the red squirrel
Soothing lap of the waves
Dancing skylarks overhead
Vibrant colours of the sinking sun
Softness of golden sand
Magic secrets of the machair
Cackle of the corncrake
Perfume of wild honeysuckle
Romance of meadow flowers
Sweetness of heather honey
Warmth of sun on the face
Gentle harmony with ease helps the troubled mind
Pain and sorrow ease with each encounter
The nightmare of betrayal and distrust fade to a new dawn of hope
Senses awaken and allow one to dream again

Family o' mine

I should like to send you a sunbeam, or the twinkle of some bright star,
or a tiny piece of the downy fleece that clings to a cloud afar.

I should like to send you the essence of a myriad sun-kissed flowers,
or the lilting song as it floats along, of a brook through fairy bowers.

I should like to send you the dew-drops that glisten at break of day,
and then at night the eerie light that mantles the Milky Way.

I should like to send you the power that nothing can overthrow –
the power to smile and laugh the while a-journeying through life you go.

But these are mere fanciful wishes; I'll send you a Godspeed instead,
and I'll clasp your hand – then you'll understand the things I've left unsaid.

anon.

• • •

'I hold that a man should strive to his uttermost for his life's set prize'

Robert Browning

Shackleton died of a heart attack while on his way to Antarctica for his fourth expedition in his ship QUEST. He was 47 years old. His body was already on its way back to England, but his wife had it diverted back to Grytviken, South Georgia to be buried in the land he loved. He now lies in a tiny, peaceful cemetery very close to the whaling station with a few whalers, a British governor who died in an accident and an Argentine soldier killed during the Falklands war. The head of his grave is the only one that points to the south, all the others face east. On the stone there is the nine pointed star that belonged to the Shackleton family and on the reverse you can read a quote from Robert Browning- Shackleton's favourite poet - 'I hold that a man should strive to the uttermost for his life's set prize.'

The Swallow

When no words seem appropriate *written by a paediatric nurse*

I won't say, "I know how you feel" – because I don't.
I've lost parents, grandparents, aunts, uncles and friends,
but I've never lost a child.
So how can I say I know how you feel?

I won't say, "You'll get over it" – because you won't.
Life will have to go on.
The washing, cooking, cleaning, the common routine.
These chores will take your mind off your loved one,
but the hurt will still be there.

I won't say, "Your other children will be a comfort to you" –
because they may not be.
Many mothers I've talked to say that after they have lost a child,
they easily lose their temper with their remaining children.
Some even feel resentful that they're alive and healthy
when the other child is not.

I won't say, "Never mind, you're young enough to have another baby"
– because that won't help.
A new baby cannot replace the one that you've lost.
A new baby will fill your hours, keep you busy,
give you sleepless nights.
But it will not replace the one you've lost.

You may hear all these platitudes from your friends and relatives.
They think they are helping.
They don't know what else to say.
You will find out who your true friends are at this time.
Many will avoid you because they can't face you.
Others will talk about the weather,
the holidays and the school concert
but never about how you're coping.

So what will I say?

I will say, "I'm here. I care. Anytime. Anywhere."
I will talk about your loved one.
We'll laugh about the good memories.
I won't mind how long you grieve.
I won't tell you to pull yourself together.
No, I don't know how you feel - but with sharing,
perhaps I will learn a little of what you are going through.
And perhaps you'll feel comfortable with me
and find your burden has eased. Try me.

• • •

High Flight
by Fl. Officer John Gillespie Magee 1922-1941

Oh, I have slipped the surly bonds of earth
And danced the skies on laughter-silvered wings.
Sunward I've climbed and joined the tumbling mirth
Of sun-split clouds - and done a hundred things
You have not dreamed of; wheeled and soared and swung
High in the sunlit silence. Hovering there
I've chased the shouting wind along, and flung
My eager craft through footless halls of air;
Up, up the long delirious burning blue
I've topped the windswept heights with easy grace,
Where never lark nor even eagle flew;
And while, with silent lifting mind I've trod
The high, untrespassed sanctity of space
Put out my hand and touched the face of God.

• • •

Two Horses in a Field

Just up the road from my home is a field, with two horses in it. From a distance, each looks like every other horse. But if one stops the car, or is walking by, one will notice something quite amazing. Looking into the eyes of one horse will disclose that he is blind. His owner has chosen not to have him put down, but has made a good home for him. This alone is amazing.

Listening, one will hear the sound of a bell. Looking around for the source of the sound, one will see that it comes from the smaller horse in the field. Attached to her bridle is a small bell. It lets her blind friend know where she is, so he can follow her.

As one stands and watches these two friends, one sees how she is always checking on him, and that he will listen for her bell and then slowly walk to where she is, trusting that she will not lead him astray.

Like the owners of these two horses, God does not throw us away just because we are not perfect or because we have problems or challenges. He watches over us and even brings others into our lives to help us when we are in need. Sometimes we are the blind horse being guided by God and those whom He places in our lives. Other times we are the guide horse, helping others see God. *anon.*

• • •

Know the true value of time; snatch, seize, and enjoy every moment of it. No idleness, no delay, no procrastination; never put off 'til tomorrow what you can do today.

Lord Chesterfield 1694-1773

Old Irish Blessing

May your day be filled with blessings
Like the sun that lights the sky,
And may you always have the courage
To spread your wings and fly!

• • •

The Joy of Living *by Ewan McColl*
Take me to some high place
Of heather, rock and ling;
Scatter my dust and ashes
Feed me to the wind.
So that I will be
Part of all you see,
The air you are breathing.
I'll be part of the curlew's cry
And the soaring hawk,
The blue milkwort
And the sundew hung with diamonds.
I'll be riding the gentle wind
That blows through your hair;
Reminding you how we shared
In the joy of living.

• • •

Eskimo Legend

Perhaps they are not the stars,
but rather openings in Heaven
where the love of our lost ones
pours through and shines down on us
to let us know they are happy.

• • •

The Swallow

I thank thee, God, that I have lived
by Elizabeth Craven (1750-1828)

I thank thee, God, that I have lived.
    In this great world and known its many joys;
The song of birds, the strong sweet scent of hay
    And cooling breezes in the secret dusk;
The flaming sunsets at the close of day,
    Hills, and the lonely, heather covered moors;
Music at night and the moonlight on the sea,
    The beat of waves upon the rocky shore
And wild white spray, flung high in ecstasy;
    The faithful eyes of dogs, and treasured books,
The love of kin and fellowship of friends,
    And all that makes life dear and beautiful.
I thank thee too, that there has come to me
    A little sorrow and sometimes defeat,
A little heartache and the loneliness
    That comes with parting and the word goodbye;
Dawn breaking after weary hours of pain,
    When I discovered that night's gloom must yield
And morning light break through to me again,
    Because of these and other blessings poured
Unasked upon my wonderful head.
    Because I know that there is yet to come
An even richer and more glorious life,
    And most of all, because thine only Son
Once sacrified life's loveliness for me–
    I thank thee, God, that I have lived.

• • •

A thing of beauty is a joy for ever:
Its loveliness increases; it will never
Pass into nothingness; but still will keep
A bower quiet for us, and a sleep
Full of sweet dreams, and health, and quiet breathing.

from John Keats' epic poem, Endymion, 1818

Never, never, never, never ever give up

Sir Winston Churchill

The Swallow

Inspirational Prayer *prayer of St Francis of Assisi*

Make me a channel of your peace
Where there is hatred let me bring your love;
Where there is injury, your pardon, Lord
And where there's doubt the true faith in you.

> *O master, grant that I may never seek*
> *So much to be consoled as to console*
> *To be understood as to understand*
> *To be loved as to love with all my soul.*

Make me a channel of your peace
Where there is despair in life let me bring hope,
Where there is darkness only light
And where there's sadness ever joy.

> *O master, grant that I may never seek*
> *So much to be consoled as to console*
> *To be understood as to understand*
> *To be loved as to love with all my soul.*

Make me a channel of your peace
It is in pardoning that we are pardoned
In giving to all men that we receive
And in dying that we are born to eternal life.

• • •

If tears could build a stairway
And memories a lane,
I'd walk right up to heaven
And bring you home again.

In Flanders Fields *by John McCrae 1915*

In Flanders fields the poppies blow
Between the crosses, row on row,
That mark our place; and in the sky
The larks, still bravely singing, fly
Scarce heard amid the guns below.
We are the Dead. Short days ago
We lived, felt dawn, saw sunset glow,
Loved and were loved, and now we lie,
In Flanders fields.
Take up our quarrel with the foe:
To you from failing hands we throw
The torch; be yours to hold it high.
If ye break faith with us who die
We shall not sleep, though poppies grow
In Flanders fields.

It was at Essex Farm, on the Western Front in Belgium, that Lt. Col. John McCrae, a Canadian Medical Officer, wrote "In Flanders Fields.". He worked to save the lives of soldiers during the Second Battle of Ypres, in 1915, in a Field Dressing Station, writing the poem on a page torn from his dispatch book between the arrival of wounded men. Having saved so many young soldiers lives, John McCrae himself died of pneumonia in France in 1918.

• ● •

'Another Tomorrow'

There's always another tomorrow,
However hard the day.
There's always an end to sorrow;
Time wipes our tears away.
There's always a reason for living,
Though sad your heart may be.
There's always another horizon
Beyond the one you see. *anon.*

Ask Me

Not, how did he die, but how did he live?
Not, what did he gain, but what did he give?
These are the units to measure the worth
Of a man as a man, regardless of birth.
Not what was his church, nor what was his creed
But had he befriended those really in need?
Was he ever ready, with the word of good cheer
To bring back a smile, to banish your tears?

anon.

• • •

It Shows In Your Face

You don't have to tell how you live each day,
You don't have to say if you work or play,
A tried, true barometer serves in its place,
However you live, it shows in your face.

The false, the deceit you wear in your heart
Will not stay inside where it first got its start;
For sinew and blood are a thin veil of lace'
However you live, it shows in your face.

If you have battled and won in the great game of life,
If you feel that you've conquered the sorrow and strife,
If you've played the game fair and you stand on first base,
You don't have to tell it. It shows in your face.

If your life's been unselfish and for others you live,
Not for what you get, but for what you can give,
If you live close to God in his infinite grace,
You don't have to tell it. It shows in your face. *anon.*

• • •

If it's for you, it won't go by you.

The Swallow

The Invitation *by Oriah Mountain Dreamer, Indian Elder*

It doesn't interest me what you do for a living.
I want to know what you ache for
and if you dare to dream of meeting your heart's longing.

It doesn't interest me how old you are.
I want to know if you will risk looking like a fool
for love
for your dream
for the adventure of being alive.

It doesn't interest me what planets are squaring your moon...
I want to know if you have touched the centre of your own sorrow
if you have been opened by life's betrayals or have become shrivelled and
closed from fear of further pain.

I want to know if you can sit with pain
mine or your own
without moving to hide it
or fade it
or fix it.

I want to know if you can be with joy mine or your own
if you can dance with wildness and let the ecstasy fill you to the tips of
your fingers and toes without cautioning us
to be careful
to be realistic
to remember the limitations of being human.

It doesn't interest me if the story you are telling me is true.
I want to know if you can disappoint another to be true to yourself.
If you can bear the accusation of betrayal and not betray your own soul.
If you can be faithless
and therefore trustworthy.

I want to know if you can see Beauty even when it is not pretty every day.
And if you can source your own life from its presence.

I want to know if you can live with failure yours and mine
and still stand at the edge of the lake and shout to the silver of the full
moon, 'Yes.'

It doesn't interest me to know where you live or how much money you
have. I want to know if you can get up after the night of grief and despair
weary and bruised to the bone and do what needs to be done
to feed the children.

It doesn't interest me who you know or how you came to be here.
I want to know if you will stand in the centre of the fire
with me and not shrink back.

It doesn't interest me where or what or with whom you have studied.
I want to know what sustains you from the inside when all else falls away.

I want to know if you can be alone with yourself
and if you truly like the company you keep in the empty moments.

• • •

Shoot for the moon.
Even if you miss you will
land among the stars.

It couldn't be done *by Edgar Guest (1881-1959)*

Somebody said that it couldn't be done,
But, he with a chuckle replied
That 'maybe it couldn't' but he would be one
Who wouldn't say so till he'd tried.

So he buckled right in with the trace of a grin
On his face. If he worried he hid it.
He started to sing as he tackled the thing
That couldn't be done, as he did it.

Somebody scoffed: 'Oh, you'll never do that;
At least no one we know has done it';
But he took off his coat and he took off his hat,
And the first thing we knew he'd begun it.

With a lift of his chin and a bit of a grin,
Without any doubting or quiddit,
He started to sing as he tackled the thing
That couldn't be done, and he did it.

There are thousands to tell you it cannot be done,
There are thousands to prophesy failure;
There are thousands to point out to you, one by one,
The dangers that wait to assail you.

But just buckle right in with a bit of a grin,
Just take off your coat and go to it;
Just start to sing as you tackle the thing
That cannot be done, and you'll do it

• • •

Life is too Precious...

Life is an opportunity, benefit from it.

Life is beauty, admire it.

Life is bliss, taste it.

Life is a dream, realise it.

Life is a challenge, meet it.

Life is a duty, complete it.

Life is a game, play it.

Life is a promise, fulfill it.

Life is sorrow, overcome it.

Life is a song, sing it.

Life is a struggle, accept it.

Life is a tragedy, confront it.

Life is an adventure, dare it.

Life is luck, make it.

Life is too precious, do not destroy it.

Life is life, fight for it.

Mother Theresa (1910 – 1997)

Stay with me God

Stay with me God, the night is dark!
The night is cold, my little spark
Of courage dims, the night is long –
Be with me God and make me strong.

I love a game, I love a fight,
I hate the dark, I love light!
I love my child, I love my wife –
I am no coward, I love life.

Life with its change of mood and shade,
I want to live – I'm not afraid
But me and mine are hard to part –
Oh Unknown God, lift up my heart.

You stilled the waters at Dunkirk
And saved your servants. All your work
Is wonderful, dear God; you strode
Before us down that dreadful road.

We were alone and hope had fled,
We loved our country and our dead
And could not shame them, so we stayed
The course, and we were not much afraid.

Dear God, that nightmare road! And then
That sea – we got there, we were men!
My eyes were blind, my feet were torn,
My soul sang like a bird at dawn!

I know that death is but a door –
I knew what we were fighting for –
Peace for our kids, our brothers freed,
A kinder world, a cleaner breed.

I'm but the son my mother bore,
A simple man, and nothing more,
But, God of strength and gentleness,
Be pleased to make me nothing less.

Help me again when death is near,
To mock the haggard face of fear –
That when I fall, if fall I must,
My soul may triumph in the dust. *anon.*

*Written on a scrap of paper, it fluttered into the hands of a
soldier sheltering in a slit trench, on the eve of El Alamein,
1942. A young officer waiting for the stroke of 22.00hrs when
the guns opened the battle stuffed it in his pocket.
He survived and the poem found its way into a little book
called 'Poems from the Desert'.*

• • •

May you have the hindsight to know where you've been, the foresight to know where you're going and the insight to know when you're going too far.

The Fork

There was a young woman who had been diagnosed with a terminal illness and had been given three months to live. So as she was getting her things 'in order,' she contacted her Pastor and had him come to her house to discuss certain aspects of her final wishes.

She told him which songs she wanted sung at the service, what scriptures she would like read, and what outfit she wanted to be buried in.

Everything was in order and the Pastor was preparing to leave when the young woman suddenly remembered something very important to her.

'There's one more thing,' she said excitedly.

'What's that?' came the Pastor's reply.

'This is very important,' the young woman continued. 'I want to be buried with a fork in my right hand.'

The Pastor stood looking at the young woman, not knowing quite what to say.

'That surprises you, doesn't it?' the young woman asked.

'Well, to be honest, I'm puzzled by the request,' said the Pastor.

The young woman explained. 'My grandmother once told me this story, and from that time on I have always tried to pass along its message to those I love and those who are in need of encouragement. In all my years of attending socials and dinners, I always remember that when the dishes of the main course were being cleared, someone would inevitably lean over and say, 'Keep your fork.' It was my favourite part because I knew that something better was coming... like velvety chocolate cake or deep-dish apple pie. Something wonderful, and with substance!'

So, I just want people to see me there in that casket with a fork in my hand and I want them to wonder 'What's with the fork?' Then I want you to tell them: 'Keep your fork, the best is yet to come."

• • •

If the only prayer you ever say in your entire life is 'thank you' it will be enough.

May you have warm words
of a cold evening;
a full moon on a dark night,
and the road downhill
all the way to your door.

• • •

Risk

To *laugh* is to risk appearing the fool.
To *weep* is to risk appearing sentimental.
To *reach out for another* is to risk involvement.
To *expose your feelings* is to risk exposing your true self.
To *place your ideas and your dreams before a crowd* is to risk their loss.
To *love* is to risk not being loved in return.
To *live* is to risk dying.
To *hope* is to risk despair.
To *try* is to risk failure.

**But risks must be taken, for the greater hazard
is to risk nothing.
The person who risks nothing, does nothing,
has nothing and is nothing.
He may avoid suffering and sorrow but he cannot learn,
change, grow, love, live.
Chained by his attitude, he is a slave, he has forfeited freedom.
Only a person who risks is free.**

The Swallow

Jonathon Livingston Seagull *by Richard Bach*

They came in the evening and found Jonathan gliding peaceful and alone through his beloved sky. The two gulls that appeared on his wings were pure as starlight, and the glow from them was gentle and friendly in the high night air. But most lovely of all was the skill with which they flew, their wingtips moving a precise and constant inch from his own.

Without a word, Jonathan put them to his test, a test that no gull had ever passed. He twisted his wings, slowed to a single mile per hour above stall. The two radiant birds slowed with him, smoothly, locked in position, they knew about slow flying.

He folded his wings, rolled, and dropped in a dive to a hundred and ninety miles per hour. They dropped with him, streaking down in flawless formation. At last he turned that speed straight up into a long vertical slow-roll. They rolled with him, smiling. He recovered to level flight and was quiet for a time before he spoke. 'Very well' he said, 'who are you?'

'We're from your Flock, Jonathan. We are your brothers.' The words were strong and calm.
'We've come to take you higher, to take you home.'
'Home, I have none. I am an Outcast. And we fly now at the peak of the Great Mountain Wind. Beyond a few hundred feet, I can lift this old body no higher.' 'But you can Jonathan. For you have learned. One school is finished, and the time has come for another to begin.'

As it had shined across him all his life, so understanding lighted that moment for Jonathan Seagull. They were right. He could fly higher, and it was time to go home. He gave one last look across the sky, across that magnificent silver land where he had learned so much.
'I'm ready' he said at last.

And Jonathan Livingston Seagull rose with the two star bright gulls to disappear into a perfect dark sky.

• • •

Life Goes On *by Joyce Grenfell (1910-1979)*

If I should go before the rest of you,
Break not a flower,
Nor inscribe a stone,
Nor, when I am gone,
Speak in a Sunday voice,
But be the usual selves
That I have known.

Weep if you must:
Parting is hell,
But life goes on,
So… sing as well."

• • •

To the living, I am gone
To the sorrowful, I will never return
To the angry, I was cheated
But to the happy, I am at peace
And to the faithful, I have never left
I cannot speak, but I can listen
I cannot be seen, but I can be heard
So as you stand upon the shore
Gazing at the beautiful sea, remember me
As you look in awe at a mighty forest
And in its grand majesty, remember me,
Remember me in your hearts,
In your thoughts, and the memories of the
Times we loved, the times we cried,
the battle we fought and the times we laughed
For if you always think of me,
I will never have gone.
anon.

• • •

A Little Inspiration *anon.*

When I was quite young, my father had one of the first telephones in our neighborhood. I remember well the polished old case fastened to the wall. The shiny receiver hung on the side of the box. I was too little to reach the telephone, but used to listen with fascination when my mother used to talk to it.

Then I discovered that somewhere inside the wonderful device lived an amazing person – her name was "Information Please" and there was nothing she did not know. "Information Please" could supply anybody's number and the correct time.

My first personal experience with this genie-in-the-bottle came one day while my mother was visiting a neighbor. Amusing myself at the tool bench in the basement, I whacked my finger with a hammer.

The pain was terrible, but there didn't seem to be any reason in crying because there was no one home to give sympathy. I walked around the house sucking my throbbing finger, finally arriving at the stairway.

The telephone!

Quickly, I ran for the footstool in the parlor and dragged it to the landing. Climbing up, I unhooked the receiver in the parlor and held it to my ear. "Information Please," I said into the mouthpiece just above my head. A click or two and a small clear voice spoke into my ear. "Information." "I hurt my finger. . ." I wailed into the phone. The tears came readily enough now that I had an audience. "Isn't your mother home?" came the question. "Nobody's home but me." I blubbered, "Are you bleeding?" "No," I replied. "I hit my finger with the hammer and it hurts." "Can you open your icebox?" she asked. I said I could. "Then chip off a little piece of ice and hold it to your finger," said the voice.

After that, I called "Information Please" for everything. I asked her for help with my geography and she told me where Philadelphia was. She helped me with my maths. She told me my pet chipmunk that I had caught in the park just the day before would eat fruits and nuts. Then, there was the time Petty, our pet canary died. I called "Information Please" and told her the sad story. She listened, then said the usual things grown-ups say to soothe a child. But I was UN-consoled. I asked her, "Why is it that birds should sing so beautifully and bring joy to all families, only to end up as a heap of feathers on the bottom of a cage?"

She must have sensed my deep concern, for she said quietly, "Paul, always remember that there are other worlds to sing in." Somehow I felt better.

Another day I was on the telephone. "Information Please."

"Information," said the now familiar voice.

"How do you spell fix?" I asked.

All this took place in a small town in the Pacific Northwest. When I was 9 years old, we moved across the country to Boston. I missed my friend very much. "Information Please" belonged in that old wooden box back home, and somehow never thought of trying the tall, shiny new phone that sat on the table in the hall.

As I grew into my teens, the memories of those childhood conversations never really left me. Often, in moments of doubt and perplexity I would recall the serene sense of security I had then. I appreciated now how patient, understanding, and kind she was to have spent her time on a little boy.

A few years later, on my way west to college, my plane put down in Seattle. I had about half an hour or so between planes. I spent 15 minutes or so on the phone with my sister, who lived there now. Then without thinking what I as doing, I dialed my hometown operator and said, "Information, Please." Miraculously, I heard the small, clear voice I knew so well, Information."

I hadn't planned this but I heard myself saying, "Could you please tell me how to spell fix?"

There was a long pause. Then came the soft spoken answer, "I guess your finger must have healed by now."

I laughed. "So it's really still you,' I said. "I wonder if you have any idea how much you meant to me during that time."

"I wonder," she said, "if you know how much your calls meant to me." "I never had any children, and I used to look forward to your calls."

I told her how often I had thought of her over the years and I asked if I could call her again when I came back to visit my sister.

"Please do, she said. "Just ask for Sally."

Three months later I was back in Seattle. A different voice answered "Information." I asked for Sally.

"Are you a friend?" She said.

"Yes, a very old friend," I answered.

"I'm sorry to have to tell you this, she said. Sally had been working part-time the last few years because she was sick. She died five weeks ago." Before I could hang up she said, "Wait a minute. Did you say your name was Paul?"

"Yes."

"Well, Sally left a message for you. She wrote it down in case you called. Let me read it to you." The note said, "Tell him I still say there are other worlds to sing in. He'll know what I mean."

I thanked her and hung up. I knew what Sally meant.

Never underestimate the impression you may make on others.

• • •

What does not destroy me, makes me strong.

• • •

Basil of Caesarea

Steer the ship of my life, good Lord, to your quiet harbour,
where I can be safe from the storms of sin and conflict.
Show me the course I should take. Renew in me the gift of discernment,
so that I can always see the right direction in which I should go.
And give me the strength and the courage to choose the right course, even
when the sea is rough and the waves are high,
knowing that through enduring hardship and danger in your name
we shall find comfort and peace.

I would be true,
for there are those who trust me;
I would be pure,
for there are those that care.
I would be strong,
for there is much to suffer;
I would be brave,
for there is much to dare.

I would be friend to all
– the foe, the friendless;
I would be giving,
and forget the gift.
I would be humble,
for I know my weakness;
I would look up
– and laugh – and live.

Howard Arnold Walter, 1906

The Swallow

Remember *by Christina Rossetti (1830-1894)*

Remember me when I am gone away,
Gone far away into the silent land;
When you can no more hold me by the hand,
Nor I half turn to go, yet turning stay.

Remember me when no more day by day
You tell me of our future that you plann'd:
Only remember me; you understand
It will be late to counsel then or pray.

Yet if you should forget me for a while
And afterwards remember, do not grieve:
For if the darkness and corruption leave
A vestige of the thoughts that once I had,
Better by far you should forget and smile
Than that you should remember and be sad.

• • •

*I have joined old friends in a golden light
Beyond yon horizon 'tis wondrous bright
It is heavenly bliss without bodily pain
So keep faith and keep strong
until we meet again*

anon.

• • •

The Window

Two men, both seriously ill, occupied the same hospital room. One man was allowed to sit up in his bed for an hour each afternoon to help drain the fluid from his lungs. His bed was next to the room's only window. The other man had to spend all his time flat on his back.

The men talked for hours on end. They spoke of their wives and families, their homes, their jobs, their involvement in the military service, where they had been on holiday.

Every afternoon when the man in the bed by the window could sit up, he would pass the time by describing to his roommate all the things he could see outside the window. The man in the other bed began to live for those one hour periods where his world would be broadened and enlivened by all the activity and colour of the world outside.

The window overlooked a park with a lovely lake. Ducks and swans played on the water while children sailed their model boats. Young lovers walked arm in arm amidst flowers of every colour and a fine view of the city skyline could be seen in the distance. As the man by the window described all this in exquisite detail, the man on the other side of the room would close his eyes and imagine the picturesque scene. One warm afternoon the man by the window described a parade passing by. Although the other man couldn't hear the band – he could see it. In his mind's eye as the gentleman by the window portrayed it with descriptive words.

Days and weeks passed. One morning, the day nurse arrived to bring water for their baths only to find the lifeless body of the man by the window, who had died peacefully in his sleep. She was saddened and called the hospital attendants to take the body away. As soon as it seemed appropriate, the other man asked if he could be moved next to the window. The nurse was happy to make the switch, and after making sure he was comfortable, she left him alone. Slowly, painfully, he propped himself up on one elbow to take his first look at the real world outside. He strained to slowly turn to look out the window beside the bed. It faced a blank wall.

The man asked the nurse what could have compelled his deceased roommate who had described such wonderful things outside this window. The nurse responded that the man was blind and could not even see the wall. She said, "Perhaps he just wanted to encourage you."

The Mayonnaise and the Coffee Jar *anon.*

When things in your life seem almost too much to handle, when 24 hours in a day are not enough, remember the mayonnaise jar and the coffee.

A professor stood before his philosophy class and had some items in front of him. When the class began, wordlessly, he picked up a very large and empty mayonnaise jar and proceeded to fill it with golf balls. He then asked the students if the jar was full.

They agreed that it was.

So the professor then picked up a box of pebbles and poured them into the jar. He shook the jar lightly. The pebbles rolled into the open areas between the golf balls. He then asked the students again if the jar was full.

They agreed it was.

The professor next picked up a box of sand and poured it into the jar. Of course, the sand filled up everything else. He asked once more if the jar was full.

The students responded with a unanimous "yes."

The professor then produced two cups of coffee from under the table and poured the entire contents into the jar, effectively filling the empty space between the sand. The students laughed. "Now," said the professor, as the laughter subsided, "I want you to recognise that this jar represents your life. The golf balls are the important things – your family, your children, your health, your friends, and your favourite passions – things that if everything else was lost and only they remained, your life would still be full.

The pebbles are the other things that matter like your job, your house, your car.

The sand is everything else – the small stuff."

If you put the sand into the jar first," he continued, "there is no room for the pebbles or the golf balls. The same goes for life. If you spend all your time and energy on the small stuff, you will never have room for the things that are important to you. "Pay attention to the things that are critical to your happiness. Play with your children. Take time to get medical checkups. Take your partner out to dinner. Play another 18 holes. There will always be time to clean the house, and fix the disposal. Take care of the golf balls first, the things that really matter. Set your priorities. The rest is just sand."

One of the students raised her hand and inquired what the coffee represented.

The professor smiled. "I'm glad you asked," he said. "It just goes to show you that no matter how full your life may seem, there's always room for a cup of coffee with a friend."

• • •

When one door of opportunity closes, another opens, but often we look so long at the closed door that we do not see the one which has been opened for us.

• • •

Commitment

'Until one is committed, there is hesitancy, the chance to
draw back, always ineffectiveness, concerning all acts of
initiative (and creation). There is one elementary truth
the ignorance of which kills countless ideas and splendid
plans: that the moment one definitely commits oneself
then providence moves too. All sorts of things occur to
help one that would never otherwise have occurred. A
whole stream of events issue from the decision, raising
in one's favour all manner of unforeseen incidents and
meetings and material assistance which no man could
have dreamed would have come his way. Whatever you
can do or dream you can do, begin it. Boldness has
genius, power and magic in it. Begin it now!'
Goethe (1749-1832)

• • •

'*Like all great travellers,
I have seen more than I remember,
and remember more than I have seen.*'

Benjamin Disraeli

• • •

'He who binds to himself a joy
Does the winged life destroy.
But he who kisses the joy as it flies
Lives in eternity's sun rise.'
William Blake

When you have gone so far that you can't manage one more step, then you've gone just half the distance that you're capable of. *Greenland Proverb*

The Swallow

Stiffen your Legs and Brace your Back *by Ken Dakers*
Gamekeeper at Kilrie and Ralia

Then stiffen your legs, and brace your back
And take my word it is true
If the man in front has got you weak
He is just as tired as you
He can't attack through a gruelling fight
And finish as he began.
He's done more work than you today,
You're just as good a man;
So, summon your last reserves of pluck –
He's careless with his chin –
You'll put it across him every time
Go in! Go in! Go in!

• • •

There was a Knight, a most distinguished man,
Who from the day on which he first began,
To ride abroad had followed chivalry,
Truth, honor, generousness and courtesy...
And though so much distinguished,
he was wise,
And in his bearing modest as a maid,
He never yet a boorish thing had said
In all his life to any, come what might:
He was a true, a perfect gentle-knight

from The Canterbury Tales by Chaucer

I remember, I remember *by Thomas Hood (1799-1845)*

I remember, I remember,
The house where I was born,
The little window where the sun
Came peeping in at morn;
He never came a wink too soon,
Nor brought too long a day,
But now, I often wish the night
Had borne my breath away!

I remember, I remember,
The roses, red and white,
The vi'lets, and the lily-cups,
Those flowers made of light!
The lilacs where the robin built,
And where my brother set
The laburnum on his birthday,--
The tree is living yet!

I remember, I remember,
Where I was used to swing,
And thought the air must rush as fresh
To swallows on the wing;
My spirit flew in feathers then,
That is so heavy now,
And summer pools could hardly cool
The fever on my brow!

I remember, I remember,
The fir trees dark and high,
I used to think their slender tops
Were close against the sky:
It was a childish ignorance,
But now 'tis little joy
To know I'm farther off from heav'n
Than when I was a boy.

A Child Loaned *by Edgar Albert Guest*

"I'll lend you for a little time
A child of Mine," He said,
"For you to love the while he lives,
And mourn for when he's dead.
It may be six or seven years
Or twenty-two or three,
But will you, till I call him back,
Take care of him for Me?
He'll bring his charms to gladden you,
And should his stay be brief,
You'll have his lovely memories
As solace for your grief."

"I cannot promise he will stay,
Since all from earth return.
But there are lessons taught down there
I want this child to learn.
I've looked this wide world over,
In my search for teachers true.
And from the throngs that crowd life's lanes,
I have selected you.
Now will you give him all your love,
Not think the labour vain,
Nor hate Me when I come to call
And take him back again?"

I fancied that I heard them say,
"Dear Lord, Thy will be done,
For all the joy Thy child shall bring,
The risk of grief we'll run.
We'll shelter him with tenderness,
We'll love him while we may,
And for the happiness we've known,
Forever grateful stay.
But should the angels call for him,
Much sooner than we planned,
We'll brave the bitter grief that comes,
And try to understand."

Some people just can't help making a
difference in our lives
By simply being who they are,
They make the world a little brighter,
a little warmer,
a little gentler,
and when they're gone we realise
how lucky we are to have known them.

• • •

66 Love is a temporary madness. It erupts like an earthquake
and then subsides. And when it subsides you have to make
a decision. You have to work out whether your roots have
become so entwined together that it is inconceivable that
you should ever part. Because this is what love is. Love is not
breathlessness, it is not excitement, it is not the promulgation
of promises of eternal passion. That is just being 'in love' which
any of us can convince ourselves we are. Love itself is what is
left over when being in love has burned away, and this is both
an art and a fortunate accident. Your mother and I had it, we
had roots that grew towards each other underground, and
when all the pretty blossom had fallen from our branches
we found that we were one tree and not two. 99

from **Captain Corelli's Mandolin** *by Louis de Bernieres*

• • •

The Owl

for wisdom

A wise old owl lived in an oak
The more he saw the less he spoke
The less he spoke the more he heard.
Why can't we all be like that wise old bird?

The Owl

If you Stand very Still

If you stand very still in the heart of a wood
you will hear many wonderful things.
The snap of a twig and the wind in the trees
and the whirl of invisible wings.

If you stand very still in the turmoil of life
and you wait for the voice from within,
you'll be led down the way of wisdom and peace,
through the rough world of chaos and din.

If you stand very still and hold onto your faith
you will get all the help that you ask.
You will draw from the silence the things that you need –
hope and courage and strength for your task. *anon.*

I walked a mile with Pleasure;
        She chatted all the way.
But left me none the wiser
        For all she had to say.

I walked a mile with Sorrow
        And ne'er a word said she
But oh, the things I learnt from her
        When Sorrow walked with me!

Robert Browning (1812 - 1889)

A Time for Everything

There is a time for everything,
And a season for every activity under heaven:
A time to be born and a time to die
A time to plant and a time to uproot,
A time to kill and a time to heal,
A time to tear down and a time to build,
A time to weep and a time to laugh,
A time to mourn and a time to dance,
A time to scatter stones and a time to gather them,
A time to embrace and a time to refrain,
A time to search and a time to give up,
A time to keep and a time to throw away,
A time to tear and a time to mend,
A time to be silent and a time to speak,
A time to love and a time to hate,
A time for war and a time for peace. *Ecclesiastes 3:1-8.*

Leisure
by William Henry Davies (1871 - 1940)

What is this life if, full of care
      We have no time to stand and stare?
No time to stand beneath the boughs
      And stare as long as sheep, or cows.
No time to see, when woods we pass,
      Where squirrels hide their nuts in grass.
No time to see, in broad daylight,
      Streams full of stars, like skies at night.
No time to turn at Beauty's glance,
      And watch her feet, how they can dance.
No time to wait till her mouth can
      Enrich that smile her eyes began.
A poor life this, if full of care,
      We have no time to stand and stare.

The Owl

From Parent to Child

I gave you life but I cannot live it for you.
I can teach you things but I cannot make you learn.
I can give you direction but I cannot push you there.
I can allow you freedom but I cannot account for it.
I can take you to church but I cannot make you believe.
I can teach you right from wrong but I cannot decide for you.
I can buy you beautiful clothes but I cannot make you beautiful inside.
I can teach you to respect but I cannot force you to show honour.
I can offer you advice but I cannot take it for you.

I can give you love but I cannot force it upon you.
I can teach you to share but I cannot make you unselfish.
I can advise you about your friends but I cannot choose them for you.
I can explain about the facts of life but I cannot build your reputation.
I can tell you about drugs but I cannot say No for you.
I can warn you about sin but I cannot make your morals.
I can help you set goals but I cannot achieve them for you.
I can teach you about kindness but I cannot force you to be gracious.
I can pray for you but I cannot make you walk with God.
I can tell you how to live but I cannot give you eternal life.

Every morning, lean thine arms
awhile upon the windowsill of heaven
and gaze upon thy God, then,
with the vision in thy heart,
turn, strong to meet the day.

After a While... Comes the Dawn
by Veronica A. Shoffstall (written age 19)

After a while you learn
the subtle difference between
holding a hand and chaining a soul
and you learn
that love doesn't mean leaning
and company doesn't always mean security.
And you begin to learn
that kisses aren't contracts
and presents aren't promises
and you begin to accept your defeats
with your head up and your eyes ahead
with the grace of woman, not the grief of a child
and you learn
to build all your roads on today
because tomorrow's ground is
too uncertain for plans
and futures have a way of falling down
in mid-flight.
After a while you learn
that even sunshine burns
if you get too much
so you plant your own garden
and decorate your own soul
instead of waiting for someone
to bring you flowers.
And you learn that you really can endure
you really are strong
you really do have worth
and you learn
and you learn
with every goodbye, you learn

The Owl

If... *by Rudyard Kipling*

If you can keep your head when all about you
Are losing theirs and blaming it on you,
If you can trust yourself when all men doubt you,
But make allowance for their doubting too;
If you can wait and not be tired by waiting,
Or being lied about, don't deal in lies,
Or being hated, don't give way to hating,
And yet don't look too good, nor talk too wise:

  If you can dream - and not make dreams your master;
  If you can think - and not make thoughts your aim;
  If you can meet with Triumph and Disaster
  And treat those two impostors just the same;
  If you can bear to hear the truth you've spoken
  Twisted by knaves to make a trap for fools,
  Or watch the things you gave your life to, broken,
  And stoop and build 'em up with worn-out tools:

If you can make one heap of all your winnings
And risk it on one turn of pitch-and-toss,
And lose, and start again at your beginnings
And never breathe a word about your loss;
If you can force your heart and nerve and sinew
To serve your turn long after they are gone,
And so hold on when there is nothing in you
Except the Will which says to them: 'Hold on!'

  If you can talk with crowds and keep your virtue,
  Or walk with Kings - nor lose the common touch,
  If neither foes nor loving friends can hurt you,
  If all men count with you, but none too much;
  If you can fill the unforgiving minute
  With sixty seconds' worth of distance run,
  Yours is the Earth and everything that's in it,
  And - which is more - you'll be a Man, my son!

The Dash *by Linda Ellis*

I read of a man who stood to speak
    At the funeral of a friend.
He referred to the dates on her tombstone
    From the beginning to the end.
He noted that first came the date of her birth
    And spoke of the following date with tears,
But he said what mattered most of all
    Was the dash between those years.
For that dash represents all the time
    That she spent alive on earth
And now only those who loved her
    Know what that little line is worth.
For it matters not how much we own,
    The cars, the house, the cash,
What matters is how we live and love
    And how we spend our dash.
So think about this long and hard;
    Are there things you'd like to change?
For you never know how much time is left
    That can still be rearranged.
If we could just slow down enough
    To consider what's true and real
And always try to understand
    The way other people feel.
And be less quick to anger
    And show appreciation more
And love the people in our lives
    Like we've never loved before
If we treat each other with respect
    And more often wear a smile,
Remembering that this special dash
    Might only last a little while.
So when your eulogy is being read
    With your life's actions to rehash
Would you be proud of the things they say
    About how you spent your dash?

> *A mother is only ever as happy as her least happy child.*

The Interview with God

I dreamed I had an interview with God.

'So you would like to interview me?' God asked.

'If you have the time' I said.

God smiled. 'My time is eternity.'
'What questions do you have in mind for me?'

'What surprises you most about human kind?'

God answered…
'That they get bored with childhood,
they rush to grow up, and then long to be children again.'

'That they lose their health to make money…
and then lose their money to restore their health.'

'That by thinking anxiously about the future,
they forget the present, such that they live in neither
the present nor the future.'

'That they live as if they will never die,
and die as though they had never lived.'

God's hand took mine and we were silent for a while.
And then I asked…
'As a parent, what are some of life's lessons
you want your children to learn?'

'To learn they cannot make anyone love them.
All they can do is let themselves be loved.'

'To learn that it is not good
to compare themselves to others.'

'To learn to forgive by practising forgiveness.'

'To learn that it only takes a few seconds
to open profound wounds in those they love,
and it can take many years to heal them.'

'To learn that a rich person
is not one who has the most,
but is one who needs the least.'

'To learn that there are people
who love them dearly,
but simply have not yet learned
how to express or show their feelings.'

'To learn that two people can
look at the same thing
and see it differently.'

'To learn that it is not enough
that they forgive one another,
but they must also forgive themselves.'

'Thank you for your time,' I said humbly.
'Is there anything else you would like
your children to know?'

God smiled and said,
'Just know that I am here... always.' *anon.*

The Owl

It Takes a Lifetime to Learn how to Live

It takes a lifetime to learn how to live,
How to share and how to give,
How to face tragedy that comes your way,
How to find courage to face each new day.
How to smile when your heart is sore,
How to go on when you can take no more.
How to laugh when you want to cry,
How to be brave when you say goodbye.
How to still love when your loss is so great,
How to forgive when your urge is to hate.
How to be sure that God's really there,
How to find Him?
Seek Him in prayer. *anon.*

- ❧ -

Whispers

The man whispered, "God speak to me." And a
    meadow-lark sang. But the man did not hear.

So the man yelled, "God speak to me." And the
    thunder rolled across the sky. But the man did not listen.

The man looked around and said, "God let me see you."
    And a star shone brightly. But the man did not see.

And the man shouted, "God show me a miracle."
    And a life was born. But the man did not notice.

So the man cried out in despair, " Touch me God,
    and let me know you are here."

Whereupon God reached down and touched the man.
    But the man brushed the butterfly away and walked on. *anon.*

Alive!

Think freely; practice patience; smile often;
Savour special moments; live God's message
Make new friends; discover old ones;
Tell those you love that you do; feel deeply.

> Forget troubles; forgive an enemy;
> Pick snowdrops; keep a promise;
> Look for rainbows; gaze at stars;
> See beauty everywhere; work hard; be wise;
> Try to understand; take time for others;
> Make time for yourself.

Laugh heartily; spread joy; take a chance;
Reach out; let someone in;
Try something new; slow down;
Be soft sometimes; believe in yourself;
Trust others; see a sunrise; listen to rain;
Reminisce; cry when you need to. *anon.*

God grant me the Serenity to accept things
I cannot change
Courage to change the things I can,
And Wisdom to know the difference.

The Loom of Time

A man's life is laid in a loom of time
To a pattern he does not see.
While the Weaver works and the shuttles fly
Till the end of eternity.

      Some shuttles are filled with silver thread,
      And some with threads of gold;
      While often but the darker hue
      Is all that they may hold.

But the weaver watches with skilful eye
Each shuttle fly to and fro,
And sees the pattern so deftly wrought
As the loom works sure and slow.

      God surely planned that pattern
      Each thread – the dark and the fair –
      Was chosen by his master skill
      And placed in the web with care.

He only knows the beauty,
And guides the shuttles which hold
The threads so unattractive,
As well as the threads of gold.

      Not till the loom is silent,
      And the shuttles cease to fly,
      Shall God unroll the pattern
      And explain the reason why

The dark threads are as needful
In the weavers skilful hand
As the threads of gold and silver
In the pattern he had planned. *anon.*

The Hill

A travelling man sat down to rest from his journey by the side of the road. As he rested, another man passed by. This other man, the traveller observed, walked very slow and was bent forward, his expression was troubled and pain reflected in his eyes.

'What ails you, fellow?' called up the wise, but simple man. 'Come and join me and take a rest, for your form is such that I see a need in you to share the burden that you carry.'

The other man sat down, stared far into the distance for a while and then began.

'I have lost the very dearest person known to me.' Tears welled up in his eyes as he spoke, he then fell silent for a short time before continuing. 'I feel that I am constantly walking up a hill and that the wind is always against me, my feet are as heavy as clay and in my stomach I carry hot coals. I say to myself now that I must turn back to ease this pain. If I walk back down the hill then maybe I will find that all of this is not true and that my loved one will be waiting to greet me.'

The traveller sat listening to the other man's story, and replied. 'You must not go back down the hill. You need to reach the top, for thereafter you will find the path will level, the wind will soften, your feet grow lighter and the hot coals will cool. To go back down the hill will prolong your pain, for the path to your healing is forward and up the hill.'

As the traveller got up to continue his journey, he said to the other man, 'The one you have lost is not at the bottom of the hill but with you all the time, for you carry their spirit in your heart.' *anon.*

The most wasted of days is one without laughter

E.E.Cummings(1894-1962)

The Owl

Death is nothing at all
by Canon Henry Scott-Holland (1847-1918)

Death is nothing at all

I have only slipped away into the next room

I am I and you are you

Whatever we were to each other

That we are still

Call me by my old familiar name

Speak to me in the easy way you always used

Put no difference into your tone

Wear no forced air of solemnity or sorrow

Laugh as we always laughed

At the little jokes we always enjoyed together

Play, smile, think of me, pray for me

Let my name be ever the household word that it always was

Let it be spoken without effort

Without the ghost of a shadow in it

Life means all that it ever meant

It is the same as it ever was

There is absolute unbroken continuity

What is death but a negligible accident?

Why should I be out of mind

Because I am out of sight?

I am waiting for you for an interval

Somewhere very near

Just around the corner

All is well.

Nothing is past; nothing is lost

One brief moment and all will be as it was before

How we shall laugh at the trouble of parting when we meet again!

Always keep a green branch in your heart, and one day a bird will come and perch on it and sing for you. Chinese Proverb

Twelve things to remember...

1   The value of time.

2   The success of perseverance.

3   The pleasure of working.

4   The dignity of simplicity.

5   The worth of character.

6   The power of kindness.

7   The influence of example.

8   The obligation of duty.

9   The wisdom of economy.

10 The virtue of patience.

11 The improvement of talent.

12 The joy of originating.

Be not afflicted
In Heaven.
I think of you.
I love you,
and, as in life, I am
still with you. *St Bonaventure*

Desiderata *by Max Ehrman (1872- 1945)*

Go placidly amidst the noise and haste
and remember what peace there may be in silence
As far as possible without surrender be on good terms with all persons.
Speak your truth quietly & clearly; and listen to others, even the dull
and ignorant; they too have their story.
Avoid loud & aggressive persons, for they are vexations to the spirit.
If you compare yourself with others; you may become vain & bitter;
for always there will be greater & lesser persons than yourself.
Enjoy your achievements as well as your plans.
Keep interested in your career, however humble; it is a real
possession in the changing fortunes of time.
Exercise caution in your business affairs; for the world is full of trickery.
But let this not blind you to what virtue there is;
many persons strive for high ideals, and everywhere life is full of heroism.
Be yourself.
Especially, do not feign affection. Neither be cynical about love;
for in the face of all aridity & disenchantment it is perennial as the grass.
Take kindly the counsel of the years, gracefully surrendering the things
of youth.
Nature strength of spirit to shield you in sudden misfortune
but do not distress yourself with imaginings.
Many fears are born of fatigue and loneliness.
Beyond a wholesome discipline, be gently with yourself.
You are a child of the universe, no less than the trees and the stars;
you have a right to be here.
And whether or not it is clear to you, no doubt the universe is
unfolding as it should.
Therefore be at peace with God, whatever you conceive Him to be,
and whatever your labours and aspirations, in the noisy confusion of life
keep peace with your soul.
With all its sham, drudgery & broken dreams, it is still a beautiful world.
Be careful. Strive to be happy.

Badger's Parting Gifts *by Susan Varley*

Badger was dependable, reliable,and always ready to lend a helping paw.
He was also very old, and he knew almost everything. Badger was so old
that he knew he must soon die.

One day, as Badger was watching Mole and Frog race down the hillside, he
felt especially old and tired. He wished more than anything that he could
run with them, but he knew his old legs wouldn't let him.

It was late when he arrived home. He wished the moon good night and
closed the curtains on the cold world outside. He had his supper and then
sat down to write a letter. When he had finished, he gently rocked himself
to and fro and soon was fast asleep having a strange yet wonderful dream
like none he'd ever had before.

The following day Badger's friends gathered anxiously outside Badger's
door. They were worried because he hadn't come out to say good morning
as he always did.

Fox broke the sad news that Badger was dead and read Badger's note to
them. It simply said, "Gone down the Long Tunnel. Bye Bye, Badger."
All the animals had loved Badger, and everyone was very sad. Mole
especially felt lost, alone and desperately unhappy.

In bed that night Mole could think only of Badger. Tears rolled down his
velvety nose, soaking the blankets he clung to for comfort.

Outside it began to snow. The snow covered the countryside, but it didn't
conceal the sadness that Badger's friends felt.

Badger had always been there when anyone needed him. The animals all
wondered what they would do now that he was gone.

As spring drew near, the animals often visited each other and talked about
the days when Badger was alive.

Mole was good at using scissors, and told about the time Badger had shown him how to cut a chain of moles from a piece of folded paper.

Frog was an excellent skater. He recalled how Badger had helped him take his first slippery steps on the ice.

Fox remembered how, when he was a young cub, he could never knot his tie properly until Badger showed him how. Fox could now tie every knot ever invented.

Badger had given Mrs. Rabbit his special recipe for gingerbread and had shown her how to bake gingerbread rabbits.

Each animal had a special memory of Badger – something he had taught them to do extremely well. He had given them each a parting gift to treasure always. Using these gifts they would be able to help each other. As the last of the snow melted, so did the animals' sadness. Whenever Badger's name was mentioned, someone remembered another story that made them all smile.

One warm spring day as Mole was walking on the hillside where he'd last seen Badger, he wanted to thank his friend for his parting gift.

'Thank you, Badger,' he said softly, believing that Badger could hear him. And... somehow... Badger did.

Death is not the extinguishing of the light,
But the putting out of a lamp
Because the dawn has come.

Rabindranath Tagore (1861-1941)

The Owl

Do not Judge...

Do not judge a biography by its length,
Nor by the number of pages in it.
Judge it by the richness of its contents

Sometimes those unfinished are among the most poignant...

Do not judge a song by its duration
Nor by the number of its notes
Judge it by the way it touches and lifts the soul

Sometimes those unfinished are among the most beautiful...

And when something has enriched your life
And when its melody lingers on in your heart
Is it unfinished?
Or is it endless? *anon.*

<hr>

Blossoms are scattered by the wind
and the wind cares nothing.
But the blossoms of the heart,
no wind can touch.
And when a friend has left us
for another country and is no more seen
her beloved presence still lives in memory.
Yoshida Kenko, 1293-1350

<hr>

An old man loved, is winter with flowers.

German proverb

Drop a Pebble in the Water *by James W. Foley (1874-1939)*

Drop a pebble in the water: just a splash, and it is gone;
But there's half-a-hundred ripples circling on and on and on,
Spreading, spreading from the centre, flowing on out to the sea,
And there is no way of telling where the end is going to be.

Drop a pebble in the water: in a minute, you forget;
But there are little waves a-flowing, and there's ripples circling yet,
And those little waves a-flowing to a great big wave have grown;
You've disturbed a mighty river just by dropping in a stone.

Drop an unkind word, or careless: in a minute, it is gone;
But there are half-a-hundred ripples circling on and on and on.
They keep spreading, spreading, spreading from the center as they go,
And there is no way to stop them, once you've started them to flow.

Drop an unkind word, or careless: in a minute, you forget;
But there are little waves a-flowing and there's ripples circling yet.
And perhaps in some sad heart, a mighty wave of tears you've stirred,
And disturbed one who was happy, ere you dropped that unkind word.

Drop a word of cheer and kindness: just a flash, and it is gone;
But there are half-a-hundred ripples circling on and on and on,
Bearing hope and joy and comfort on each splashing, dashing wave,
Till you wouldn't believe the volume of the one kind word you gave.

Drop a word of cheer and kindness: in a minute, you forget;
But there's gladness still a-swelling and there's joy according yet
And you've rolled a wave of comfort whose sweet music can be heard
Over miles and miles of water, just by dropping one kind word.

Better to light a candle than to curse the darkness.

Confucius

The Owl

God has created me... *by Cardinal John Henry Newman (1801-1890)*

God has created me to do him some definite service, He has committed some work to me which He has not committed to another. I have my mission – I may never know it in this life, but I shall be told it in the next.

I am a link in a chain, a bond of connection between persons. He has not created me for naught. I shall do good, I shall do His work. I shall be an angel of peace, a preacher of truth in my own place while not intending it – if I do but keep His commandments.

Therefore I will trust Him, whatever, whenever I am, I can never be thrown away. If I am in sickness, my sickness may serve Him, in perplexity, my perplexity may serve Him, if I am in sorrow, my sorrow may serve Him. He does nothing in vain.

He knows what He is about. He may take away my friends. He may throw me among strangers. He may make me feel desolate, make my spirits sink, hide my future from me – still He knows what He is about.

Every survival kit
should contain a sense of humour

So many gods, so many creeds
So many paths that wind and wind,
While just the art of being kind,
Is all the sad world needs.
Ella Wheeler Wilcox, American poet (1850-1919)

Hold fast to the human inside and you will survive

from The Diving Bell and The Butterfly
by Jean-Dominique Bauby (1952-1997)

Jean-Dominique Bauby was the editor of the French fashion magazine Elle. In 1995, at the age of 43, Bauby suffered a massive stroke which left his entire body paralysed and speechless; yet mentally intact; he could only blink his left eyelid. Despite his condition, he wrote the book The Diving Bell and the Butterfly by blinking when the correct letter was reached by a person slowly reciting the alphabet over and over again. The book was published in 1997 and Bauby died of pneumonia ten days later.

God be in my head
And in my understanding
God be in my eyes
And in my looking
God be in my mouth
And in my speaking
God be in my heart
And in my thinking
God be at my end
And at my departing.
Sir Henry Walford Davies (1869-1941)

 Don't look for flaws as you go through life,
And even when you find them,
It is wise and kind to be somewhat blind,
And to look for the virtues behind them.

The Owl

Children Learn What They Live *by Dorothy Law Nolte (1954)*

If a child lives with criticism
he learns to condemn.

If a child lives with hostility
he learns to fight.

If a child lives with ridicule
he learns to be shy.

If a child lives with shame
he learns to feel guilty.

If a child lives with tolerance
he learns to be patient.

If a child lives with encouragement
he learns confidence.

If a child lives with praise
he learns to appreciate.

If a child lives with fairness
he learns justice.

If a child lives with security
he learns to have faith.

If a child lives with approval
he learns to like himself.

If a child lives with acceptance
and friendship he learns to
find love in the world.

If I Had My Life Over – I'd Pick More Daisies
by Nadine Stair, aged 85

If I had my life to live over, I'd dare to make more mistakes next time.
I'd relax, I would limber up. I would be sillier than I have been this trip.
I would take fewer things seriously. I would take more chances. I would
climb more mountains and swim more rivers. I would eat more ice cream
and less beans. I would perhaps have more actual troubles, but I'd have
fewer imaginary ones.

You see, I'm one of those people who lived sensibly and sanely, hour after
hour, day after day. Oh, I've had my moments, and if I had to do it over
again, I'd have more of them. In fact, I'd try to have nothing else. Just
moments, one after another, instead of living so many years ahead of each
day. I've been one of those persons who never goes anywhere without a
thermometer, a hot water bottle, a raincoat and a parachute. If I had to do
it again, I would travel lighter than I have.

If I had my life to live over, I would start barefoot earlier in the spring
and stay that way later in the fall. I would go to more dances. I would ride
more merry-go-rounds. I would pick more daisies.

66 If a man does not keep
pace with his companions,
perhaps it is because he hears
a different drummcr. Lct
him step to the music which
he hears, however measured
or far away." *Henry David Thoreau, 1817-1962*

Good and Clever
by Elizabeth Wordsworth (1840-1932)

If all the good people were clever,
And all clever people were good,
The world would be nicer than ever
We thought that it possibly could.

But somehow 'tis seldom or never
The two hit it off as they should,
The good are so harsh to the clever,
The clever, so rude to the good!

So friends, let it be our endeavour
To make each by each understood;
For few can be good, like the clever,
Or clever, so well as the good.

'Grief is the price we pay for love'

Her Majesty, The Queen - St Pauls at 9/11 service

"I wonder where my sorrows could be!"
He smiled a gentle smile and said,
"My child, they're all here with me"
I asked God, why He gave me the boxes,
Why the gold and the black with the hole?
"My child, the gold is for you to count your blessings,
The Black is for you to let go
A ball is a circle, no beginning, no end.
It keeps us together like our Circle of Friends.
But the treasure inside for you to see
Is the treasure of friendship you've granted me.

anon

Father of all mankind, make the roof of my house wide enough for all opinions, oil the door of my house so it opens easily to friend and stranger and set such a table in my house that my whole family may speak kindly and freely around it.

I hope that my child,
looking back on today
Remembers a mother
who had time to play
Children grow up
while you're not looking,
There'll be years ahead
for cleaning and cooking
So quiet now, cobwebs;
dust go to sleep
I'm rocking my baby,
and babies don't keep

'Life, believe, is not a dream
So dark as sages say;
Oft a little morning rain
Foretells a pleasant day.
Sometimes there are clouds of gloom,
But these are transient all;
If the shower will make the roses bloom.
Oh why lament its fall?'   *Charlotte Bronte(1816-1855)*

Into
every life
a little
rain
must fall

Let me do my work each day *by Max Ehrmann (1872-1945)*

Let me do my work each day; and if the darkened hours of despair overcome me, let me not forget the strength that comforted me in the desolation of other times.

> Let me still remember the bright hours that found me walking over the silent hills of my childhood, or dreaming on the margin of the quiet river, when a light glowed within me, and I promised my early God to have courage amid the tempests of the changing years.

Spare me from bitterness and from the sharp passions of unguarded moments.

> Let me not forget that poverty and riches are of the spirit. Though the world know me not, let my thoughts and actions be such as shall keep me friendly with myself.

Lift my eyes from the earth, and let me not forget the uses of the stars. Forbid that I should judge others lest I condemn myself.

> Let me not follow the clamour of the world, but walk calmly in my path. Give me a few friends who will love me for what I am; and keep ever burning before my vagrant steps the kindly light of hope.

And though age and infirmity overtake me, and I come not within sight of the castle of my dreams, teach me still to be thankful for life, and for time's golden memories which are good and sweet; and may the evening's twilight find me (courageous and gentle) still.

"Find something that you love to do
And you'll never have to work a day in your life."

Sandy McConnachie, gamekeeper at Tillypronie

A Child's Grief *by M.S. Lowndes*

Lord you care so much
For the tears of a hurting child
Who has felt the grief of tragedy
Now no longer wears a smile

> Unable to clearly express
> How much he's hurting inside
> Not fully understanding the pain
> Nor knowing the reasons 'why'

He wants so much to reach out
To someone who will listen
Someone that can hold him close
And respond with godly wisdom

> For he just needs a grown up
> To know what he's going through
> But often we don't realise his grief
> Because we are hurting too

Let him know you care Lord
And will be there when we're not
The emptiness he feels within
May be filled with you oh God

> May he know you as a father
> And know you're by his side
> To come and wipe his tears away
> When alone he silently cries

Hold him in your arms Lord
So he will be at peace
Allow us all to give him time
In dealing with his grief

> For tears may last all night
> But joy comes in the morning
> So let him grieve throughout the night
> For a new day will be dawning

Perchance

If I perchance should die
And leave thee here alone
Be not as others, sore, cast down by grief
Who keep long vigil by the dust and weep.

Take up those dear unfinished tasks of mine
And I perchance may therein comfort thee. *anon.*

~

Doctors prescribe medicines
of which they know little,
to cure diseases
of which they know less,
in human beings
of whom they know nothing.

Volaire

~

The Owl

Light up the candle
Look into the light
And know you are loved
Be well – get well
For the sake of love
And be, for you are.
Zoroastrian bidding

Lord, thou knowest better than I know myself, that I am growing older and will some day be old. Keep me from the fatal habit of thinking I must say something on every subject and on every occasion. Release me from craving to straighten out everybody's affairs. Make me thoughtful but not moody; helpful but not bossy.

With my vast store of wisdom it seems a pity not to use it all, but thou knowest Lord that I want a few friends at the end.

Keep my mind free from the recital of endless details; give me wings to get to the point. I dare not ask for an improved memory, but for a humility and a lessening cocksureness, when my memory seems to clash with the memories of others. Teach me the glorious lesson that occasionally I may be mistaken.

Keep me reasonably sweet. Give me the ability to see good things in unexpected people and give me, O Lord, the grace to tell them so.

Amen

May your neighbours respect you;
Trouble neglect you;
The angels protect you, and
Heaven accept you.

Old Irish Blessing

Cats in the Cradle *by Guns 'n' Roses*

My child arrived just the other day
He came to the world in the usual way
But there were planes to catch and bills to pay
He learned to walk while I was away
And he was talkin' 'fore I knew it
And as he grew he'd say
I'm gonna be like you, Dad,
You know I'm gonna be like you.

> My son turned ten just the other day.
> He said, 'Thanks for the ball,
> Dad. Come on, let's play.
> Can you teach me to throw?'
> I said, 'Not today. I got a lot to do.'
> He said, 'That's okay.'
> And then he walked away but his smile
> never dimmed and he said,
> 'I'm gonna be like him, yeah.
> You know I'm gonna be like him.'

I've long since retired, my son's moved away.
I called him up just the other day.
I said, 'I'd like to see you, if you don't mind.'
He said, 'I'd love to, Dad, if I could find the time.
You see my new job's a hassle and
the kids have the flu
But it's sure nice talkin' to you, Dad.
it's been sure nice talkin' to you.'
And as I hung up the phone it occurred to me,
He'd grown up just like me.
My boy was just like me.

My Life is but a Weaving

My life is but a weaving
between my Lord and me;
I cannot choose the colours,
He worketh steadily.
Oft times He weaveth sorrow,
And I, in foolish pride,
Forget He sees the upper,
And I the under side.

Not 'til the loom is silent
and the shuttles cease to fly,
Shall God unroll the canvas
and explain the reason why.
The dark threads are as needful
in the Weaver's skilful hand,
As the threads of gold and silver
in the pattern He has planned.
He knows, He loves, He cares,
nothing this truth can dim.
He gives His very best to those
who leave the choice with Him.

anon

God never dreams
of blaming a daisy
for not being a daffodil!

No bird soars too high, if he soars with his own two wings

from The Marriage of Heaven and Hell by William Blake (1757-1827)

The Owl

She is Gone...

You can shed tears that she is gone,
Or you can smile because she has lived.

You can close your eyes and pray that she will come back,
Or you can open your eyes and see all that she has left.

Your heart can be empty because you can't see her,
Or you can be full of the love that you shared.

You can turn your back on tomorrow and live yesterday,
Or you can be happy for tomorrow because of yesterday.

You can remember her and only that she is gone,
Or you can cherish her memory and let it live on.

You can cry and close your mind, be empty and turn your back,
Or you can do what she would want: smile,
open your eyes, love and go on.

Foot Note:
Included by the Queen on the order of service for the Queen Mother's funeral on Tuesday 9th April 2002, the poem 'She Is Gone' was credited to 'Anon'.

After the Queen Mother's funeral much effort went into attempts to identify the author, who was discovered to be former baker David Harkins from Cumbria.
David Harkins had written the piece in the early eighties, though not as a funeral oration, but in homage to an unrequited love. David Harkins said: "I laugh about it because death is not what it's about. It wasn't written for a funeral. I wrote it about a girl I lusted after when I was 23, but she couldn't stand the sight of me. She was 16 and didn't know me, but I had seen her about and knocked on her door one evening in November 1981. She answered, and I introduced myself as a painter (painting was a hobby of mine back then) and asked her to pose.
She agreed, and I returned on the Thursday evening, when I made feeble attempts to sketch her. This proved difficult as her mother was present throughout.
She posed for me about eight times, and we met regularly for a couple of years and talked a great deal, though we never even kissed, which is probably why I poured all my feelings about her into my poetry. It was nothing to do with anyone dying but at the same time, I am humbled by the fact that anyone should use it at a funeral, especially for the Queen Mother."

Spring will come again

Mourn not with broken heart, when dear ones go,
For you the night of loneliness, for them the morning's glow.
For you the daily burden of the years which are yet to be,
For them, a new adventure in a world you cannot see.
For sorrow has its season, nothings lasts, not even grief.
Every winter has its ending, and then the greening leaf.
One day you will awake and find that time has eased the pain
That is how God's mercy works – spring will come again.

One day at a time – this is enough.
Do not look back and grieve over
the past, for it is gone; and do not
be troubled about the future,
for it has not yet come.
Live in the present and make it
so beautiful that it will be
worth remembering.

No man is an island

No man is an island, entire in itself; every man is a piece of the continent,
a part of the main; if a clod be washed away by the sea, Europe is the less,
as well as if a promontary were, as well as if a Manor of thy friends or of
thine own were; any man's death diminishes me because I am involved in
Mankind. And therefore never send to know for whom the bell tolls; it
tolls for thee. *John Donne (1573-1631)*

The Owl

Mother Teresa's Philosophy

People are often unreasonable,
irrational, and self centered;
　Forgive them anyway.

If you are kind, people may accuse
you of selfish, ulterior motives;
　Be kind anyway

If you are successful,
you will win some
unfaithful friends and
some genuine enemies;
　Succeed anyway.

If you are honest and sincere,
people may deceive you;
Be honest and sincere anyway.

What you spend years creating
others may destroy overnight;
　Create anyway.

If you find serenity and happiness,
some may be jealous;
　Be happy anyway

The good you do today
will often be forgotten;
　Do good anyway

Give the best you have
and it may never be enough;
Give the best you have anyway.

In the final analysis
it is between you and God;
It was never between you
and them anyway.

*This poem was written by Mother Teresa
and is engraved on the wall of her home
for children in Calcutta*

Life is mostly froth and bubble
Two things stand out alone;
Kindness in another's trouble,
Courage in your own.

Our deepest fear is not that we are inadequate.
Our deepest fear is that we are powerful beyond measure.
It is our light, not our darkness, that most frightens us.
We ask ourselves, who am I to be brilliant, gorgeous,
talented and fabulous?
Actually, who are you not to be?
You are a child of God.
Your playing small doesn't serve the world.
There's nothing enlightened about shrinking
so that other people won't feel insecure around you.
We were born to make manifest the glory of God
that is within us.
It's not just in some of us, it's in everyone.
And as we let our own light shine,
we unconsciously give others permission to do the same.
As we are liberated from our own fear,
our presence automatically liberates others
Nelson Mandela – 1994 Inaugural Speech

It hath been taught us from the primal state

that he which is was wished until he were

William Shakespeare

Special People

People come into your life for a Reason, a Season, or a Lifetime.
When you know which one it is for a person,
you will know what to do for that person.

When someone is in your life for a *Reason*, it is usually to meet a need
you have expressed. They have come to assist you through a difficulty,
to provide you with guidance and support, to aid you physically,
emotionally, or spiritually. They may seem like a Godsend, and they are!
They are there for the reason you need them to be.
Then, without any wrong-doing on your part, or at an inconvenient time,
this person will say or do something to bring the relationship to an end.
Sometimes they die. Sometimes they walk away.
Some times they act up and force you to take a stand.
What we must realise is that our need has been met, our desire fulfilled,
their work is done. The prayer you sent up has been answered,
and now it is time to move on.

Some people come into your life for a *Season*,
because your turn has come to share, grow, or learn. They bring you an
experience of peace, or make you laugh. They may teach you something
you have never done. They usually give you an unbelievable amount of joy.
Believe it! It is real! But, only for a season.

Lifetime relationships teach you lifetime lessons:
things you must build upon in order to have a solid emotional foundation.
Your job is to accept the lesson,
love the person, and put what you have learned
to use in all other relationships and areas of your life.
It is said that love is blind but friendship is clairvoyant.
Thank you for being a part of my life! *anon.*

Lighten our darkness, we beseech thee, O Lord; and by thy great mercy defend us from all perils and dangers of this night; for the love of thy only Son, our Saviour Jesus Christ. Amen. *Evensong, the 3rd Collect from the Book of Common Prayer*

Patience serves as a protection against wrongs as clothes do against cold. For if you put on more clothes as the cold increases, it will have no power to hurt you. So in like manner you must grow in patience when you meet with great wrongs, and they will then be powerless to vex your mind.
Leonardo Da Vinci (1452-1519)

The air of heaven is that which blows between a horse's ears. Arabian Proverb

The Owl

Instructions for Life in the new Millennium *by The Dalai Lama*

1   Take into account that great love and great achievements involve great risk.

2   When you lose, don't lose the lesson.

3   Follow the three Rs: Respect for self, respect for others and responsibility for all your actions.

4   Remember that not getting what you want is sometimes a wonderful stroke of luck.

5   Learn the rules so you know how to break them properly.

6   Don't let a little dispute injure a great friendship.

7   When you realise you've made a mistake, take immediate steps to correct it.

8   Spend some time alone every day.

9   Open your arms to change, but don't let go of your values.

10   Remember that silence is sometimes the best answer.

11   Live a good, honourable life. Then when you get older and think back, you'll be able to enjoy it a second time.

12   A loving atmosphere in your home is the foundation for your life.

13   In disagreements with loved ones, deal only with the current situation. Don't bring up the past.

14   Share your knowledge. It's a way to achieve immortality.

15   Be gentle with the earth.

16   Once a year, go some place you've never been before.

17   Remember that the best relationship is one in which your love for each other exceeds your need for each other.

18   Judge your success by what you had to give up in order to get it.

19   Approach love and cooking with reckless abandon.

Please and *Thank You.*
Simple words which cost nothing
and pay the biggest dividend.

from The House at Pooh Corner
by AA Milne (1882-1956)

'Pooh, promise you won't forget about me, ever.
Not even when I'm a hundred.'
Pooh thought for a little.
'How old shall I be then?'
'Ninety-nine'
Pooh nodded.
'I promise,' he said.

*Pray for me as I shall for thee;
that we may love and laugh again
when we meet merrily in heaven*

Sir Thomas More (1478-1535)

from St. Paul's letter to the Colossians

Put on then, as God's chosen ones, holy and beloved, compassion,
kindness, lowliness, meekness, and patience, forbearing one
another and, if one has a complaint against another, forgiving each
other; as the Lord has forgiven you, so you also must forgive.
And above all these put on love, which binds everything together in
perfect harmony. *Chap. 3 vs. 12 - 14 (Revised Standard Version)*

Say not in grief he is no more
but live in thankfulness
that he was.

The Owl

The Guy In The Glass *by Dale Wimbrow, 1934*

When you get what you want in your struggle for pelf,
    And the world makes you King for a day,
Then go to the mirror and look at yourself,
    And see what that guy has to say.
For it isn't your Father or Mother or Wife,
    Who judgement upon you must pass.
The feller whose verdict counts most in your life,
    Is the guy staring back from the glass.
He's the feller to please, never mind all the rest,
    For he's with you clear up to the end,
And you've passed your most dangerous, difficult test
    If the guy in the glass is your friend.
You may be like Jack Horner and 'chisel' a plum,
    And think you're a wonderful guy,
But the man in the glass says you're only a bum
    If you can't look him straight in the eye.
You can fool the whole world down the pathway of years,
    And get pats on the back as you pass,
But your final reward will be heartaches and tears
    If you've cheated the guy in the glass.

- ~ -

The death of the old is like a fire sinking and going out of its own accord, without external impulsion. In the same way as apples, while green, can only be picked with force, but after ripening to maturity, fall off by themselves, so death comes to the young with violence, but to old people when the time is ripe.
The thought of this ripeness so greatly attracts me, that as I approach death I feel like a man nearing harbour after a long voyage. I seem to be catching sight of land.

Cicero

- ~ -

The Life That I Have *by Leo Marks*

The life that I have is all that I have,
And the life that I have is yours.
The love that I have of the love that I have
Is yours and yours and yours

A sleep I shall have a rest I shall have.
Yet death will be but a pause,
For the peace of my years in the long green grass
Will be yours and yours and yours.

*Leo Marks, (1920-1956) was the chief cryptographer of Special Operations
Executive during the Second World War.*

*Of all the agents that Marks briefed there is one in particular, Violette Szabo, a
French Agent with whom he will always be linked. In 1943, Marks met, and fell
in love with, a woman who lived in a neighbouring flat in the Edgware Road, but
within three months she had been killed in an air-crash in Canada. When, early
the next year, Szabo needed a code-poem for a mission in France, Marks gave her
the lines that he had written for the dead woman. Curious, Szabo asked who had
written them. 'I'll check up,' Marks told her, 'and let you know when you get back.'
In fact, as Marks had feared, Szabo never returned, but was captured, tortured and
eventually killed by the Nazis.*

*In 1958 a film of Szabo's life was made, named Carve Her Name With Pride
starring Virginia McKenna as Szabo. In the film, before kneeling down to be shot in
the back of the head (as was witnessed by another British agent in the camp), Szabo
recites the code-poem Marks had given her. On the film's release, and despite Marks's
request for anonymity, he was eventually named as the author of the poem. A recent
survey of the The Nation's 100 Favourite Poems showed that "The life that I have
is still in the Top 20".*

This too shall pass *Buddhist saying*

The Owl

Your joy is your sorrow unmasked

Your joy is your sorrow unmasked.
And the selfsame well from which your laughter rises
was oftentimes filled with your tears.
And how else can it be?
The deeper that sorrow carves into your being,
the more joy you can contain.
Is not the cup that holds your wine
the very cup that was burned in the potter's oven?
And is not the lute that soothes your spirit,
the very wood that was hollowed with knives?
When you are joyous,
look deep into your heart and you shall find it is only
that which has given you sorrow that is giving you joy.
When you are sorrowful look again in your heart,
and you shall see that in truth you are weeping for that
which has been your delight.
Some of you say, "Joy is greater than sorrow,"
and others say, "Nay, sorrow is the greater."
But I say unto you, they are inseparable.
Together they come, and when one sits alone with you at your board,
remember that the other is asleep upon your bed.
Verily you are suspended like scales between your sorrow and your joy.
Only when you are empty are you at standstill and balanced.
When the treasure-keeper lifts you to weigh his gold and his silver,
needs must your joy or your sorrow rise or fall.
Kahil Gibran: The Prophet

- ❧ -

**The most beautiful thing we can experience
is the mysterious.
It is the source of all true art and all science.
He to whom this emotion is a stranger,
who can no longer pause to wonder and stand rapt in awe,
is as good as dead: his eyes are closed.**
Albert Einstein

Success depends on three things: *Who says it, What he says, How he says it;* and of these three things, *What he says* is the least important.

John, Viscount Morley of Blackburn, Recollections

The Most Beautiful Flower

The park bench was deserted as I sat down to read.
      Beneath the long, straggly branches of an old willow tree.
Disillusioned by life with good reason to frown,
      For the world was intent on dragging me down.

And if that weren't enough to ruin my day,
      A young boy out of breath approached me, all tired from play.
He stood right before me with his head tilted down
      And said with great excitement, 'Look what I found!'

In his hand was a flower, and what a pitiful sight,
      With its petals all worn - not enough rain, or too little light.
Wanting him to take his dead flower and go off to play,
      I faked a small smile and then shifted away.

But instead of retreating he sat next to my side
      And placed the flower to his nose.
And declared with overacted surprise,
      'It sure smells pretty and it's beautiful, too.
      That's why I picked it; here, it's for you.'

The weed before me was dying or dead.
      Not vibrant of colors: orange, yellow or red.
But I knew I must take it, or he might never leave.
      So I reached for the flower, and replied, 'Just what I need.'

But instead of him placing the flower in my hand,
      He held it mid-air without reason or plan.
It was then that I noticed for the very first time,
      That weed-toting boy could not see: he was blind.

I heard my voice quiver; tears shone in the sun,
      As I thanked him for picking the very best one.
'You're welcome,' he smiled, and then ran off to play,
      Unaware of the impact he'd had on my day. *anon*.

I sat there and wondered how he managed to see
      A self-pitying woman beneath an old willow tree.
How did he know of my self-indulged plight?
      Perhaps from his heart, he'd been blessed with true sight.

Through the eyes of a blind child, at last I could see
      The problem was not with the world; the problem was me.
And for all of those times I myself had been blind,
      I vowed to see the beauty in life,
      And appreciate every second that's mine.

And then I held that wilted flower up to my nose
      And breathed in the fragrance of a beautiful rose
And smiled as I watched that young boy,
      Another weed in his hand,
      About to change the life of an unsuspecting old man. *anon.*

Take time to think, it is the source of power,
Take time to pray, it is the greatest power on earth
Take time to laugh, it is the music of the soul,
Take time to give, it is too short a life to be selfish
Take time to love and be loved, it is a God-given privilege.
T. de Chardin

Tenderhanded stroke a nettle,
And it stings you for your pains;
Grasp it like a man of mettle,
And it soft as silk remains.   *Thomas Fuller*

The Song of the River
by W.R. Hearst (1863-1951)

The snow melts on the mountain.
And the water runs down to the spring,
And the spring in a turbulent fountain,
With a song of youth to sing,
Runs down to the riotous river,
And the river flows to the sea,
And the water again
Goes back in rain
To the hills where it used to be.
And I wonder if life's deep mystery
Isn't much like the rain and the snow
Returning through all eternity
To the places it used to know.
For life was born on the lofty heights
And flows in a laughing stream,
To the river below
Whose onward flow
Ends in a peaceful dream.
And so at last,
When our life has passed
And the river has run its course,
It again goes back,
O'er the selfsame track,
To the mountain which was its source.
So why prize life
Or why fear death,
Or dread what is to be?
The river ran its alloted span
Till it reached the silent sea.
Then the water harked back
To the mountain-top
To begin its course once more.
So we shall run
The course begun

Till we reach the silent shore.
Then revisit earth
In a pure rebirth
From the heart of the virgin snow.
So don't ask why
We live or die,
Or whither, or when we go,
Or wonder about the mysteries
That only God may know.

When disaster strikes, and the world feels bleak, remember that someone, somewhere, is suffering more than you.

The best remedy for those who are afraid, lonely or unhappy is to go outside, somewhere where they can be quiet, alone with the heavens, nature and God. Because only then does one feel that all is as it should be and that God wishes to see people happy, amidst the simple beauty of nature. As long as this exists, and it certainly always will, I know that then there will always be comfort for every sorrow, whatever the circumstances may be. And I firmly believe that nature brings solace in all troubles
Anne Frank (1929-1945)

Anne Frank was a Jewish girl in Amsterdam who kept a diary while she lived with her family and others hidden in an attic from the Nazi occupiers of the Netherlands. Anne Frank died in a Nazi concentration camp in 1945. Anne Frank and her diary provide a unique insight into day-to-day life during the Nazi regime.

The Touch of the Master's Hand
by Myra Brooks Welch

'Twas battered and scarred, and the auctioneer
Thought it scarcely worth his while
To waste much time on the old violin,
But he held it up with a smile.
'What am I bidden, good folks?' he cried,
'Who will start bidding for me?
A pound", "a pound' ' then 'Two!' 'Only two?
Two pounds, once: three pounds, twice:
Going for three' ' but no,
From the room, far back, a grey-haired man
Came forward and picked up the bow:
Then, wiping the dust from the old violin,
And tightening the loose strings,
He played a melody pure and sweet
As sweet as a caroling angel sings.

The music ceased, and the auctioneer,
With a voice that was quiet and low,
Said, 'What am I bidden for the old violin?'
And he held it up with the bow.
'A thousand pounds, and who'll make it two?
Two thousand! And who'll make it three?
Three thousand, once; three thousand, twice;
And going, and gone!" said he.
The people cheered, but some of them cried
'We do not quite understand
What changed its worth?' Swift came the reply
'The touch of the master's hand'.

And many a man with life out of tune,
And battered and scattered with sin,
Is auctioned cheap to the thoughtless crowd,
Much like the old violin.
A 'mess of pottage', a glass of wine;
A game and he travels on.
He's 'going' once, and 'going' twice,
He's 'going' and 'almost gone'.
But the Master comes, and the foolish crowd
Never can quite understand
The worth of a soul and the change that's wrought
By the touch of the Master's hand.

The clock of life is wound but once
And no man has the power
To tell just when the hands will stop
At late or early hour.
Now is the only time you own.
Live, love, toil with a will.
Place no faith in time.
For the clock may soon be still. *anon.*

The Owl

Wild Geese
by Mary Oliver

You do not have to be good.
You do not have to walk on your knees
for a hundred miles through the desert repenting.
You only have to let the soft animal of your body
Love what it loves.
Tell me about your despair, yours, and I will tell you mine.
Meanwhile the sun and the clear pebbles of the rain
Are moving across the landscapes,
Over the prairies and the deep trees,
the mountains and the rivers.
Meanwhile the wild geese, high in the clean blue sky,
are heading home again.
Whoever you are, no matter how lonely,
The world offers itself to your imagination,
Calls to you like the wild geese, harsh and exciting –
Over and over announcing your place
in the family of things.

What the caterpillar calls the end of the world, the master calls a butterfly

---

The greatest pleasure of life is love,
The greatest treasure, contentment,
The greatest possession, health,
The greatest ease is sleep,
The greatest medicine is a true friend.
Sir William Temple, English statesman and essayist (1628-99)

Let Me Go
by Mabeel Easley

When I come to the end of the road,
And the sun has set on me;
I want no rites in a gloom filled room,
Why cry for a soul set free?

Miss me little - but not for long,
And not with your head bowed low.
Remember the love that we once shared,
Miss me - but let me go.

For this is a journey we all must take,
And each must go alone.
It's all part of the Master's plan,
A step on the road to home.

When you are lonely and sick at heart,
Go to the friends we know.
And bury your sorrows in doing good deeds,
Miss me - but let me go.

- ⟨⟩ -

*A fragment written by Sappho around the 6th century BC,
from Sappho, translated by Mary Barnard
(University of California Press, 1958, © renewed by Mary Barnard 1986)
no title to poem*

You may forget but

Let me tell you this:
someone in
some future time
will think of us

Living Bouquets
by Mabeel Easley

When I quit this mortal shore
    And mosey 'round this earth no more,
Do not weep and do not sob;
    I may have found a better job.
Don't go and buy a large bouquet
    For which you'll find it hard to pay,
Don't mope around and feel all blue;
    I may be better off than you.

Don't tell the folks I was a saint
    Or any old thing that I ain't.
If you have jam like that to spread,
    Please hand it out before I'm dead.
If you have roses bless your soul,
    Just pin one in my buttonhole
While I'm alive and well today;
    Don't wait until I'm gone away.

The greatest glory in living lies not in never falling, but in rising every time we fall.

Nelson Mandela

Your Children are Not Your Children
by Kahil Gibran: The Prophet

Your children are not your children.
They are the sons and daughters of Life's longing for itself.
They come through you but not from you,
And though they are with you, yet they belong not to you.
You may give them your love but not your thoughts.
For they have their own thoughts.
You may house their bodies but not their souls,
For their souls dwell in the house of tomorrow, which you
cannot visit, not even in your dreams.
You may strive to be like them, but seek not to make them
like you.
For life goes not backward nor tarries with yesterday.
You are the bows from which your children as living arrows
are sent forth.
The archer sees the mark upon the path of the infinite, and
He bends you with His might that His arrows may go swift
and far.
Let your bending in the archer's hand be for gladness;
For even as he loves the arrow that flies,
so He loves also the bow that is stable

The flower has faded
But while it bloomed
Its beauty was a joy to behold
And like the flower
Our mortal soul
Will fade, and pass away
So tarry for a while
When the flower's in bloom
And enjoy two lives as one
Gamekeeper at Kilrie and Ralia

Untitled
by Henry Longfellow

What then? Shall we sit idly down and say
The night hath come, it is no longer day?
Something remains for us to do, or dare;
Even the oldest tree some fruit may bear;
For age is opportunity no less
Than youth itself, though in another dress,
And as the evening twilight fades away
The sky is filled with stars invisible by day.

To live in the hearts of those you love is not to die anon

To be glad of life because it gives you to chance to love and to work and to play and to look up at the stars; to be satisfied with your possessions but not content with yourself until you have made the best of them; to despise nothing in the world except falsehood and meanness, and to fear nothing except cowardice; to be governed by you admirations rather than by your disgusts; to covet nothing that is your neighbour's except his kindness of heart and gentleness of manners; to think seldom of your enemies, often of your friends, and every day of Christ; to spend as much time as you can in God's out-of doors; these are the little guideposts on the footpaths to peace.
Henry Van Dyke, American writer and cleric (1852-1933)

You can't change the past,
But you can ruin the present
By worrying about the future.

Without love we are nothing; life consists in the giving
and getting of it,
For what would we know of love
if no one had loved us first?
How and where would we begin?
In time our children leave us and love elsewhere,
in a different way from the way we have loved them.
Different, but related.
With God's help, this is how life continues, its delicate
patterns interconnected by the filaments of love,
and eventually, what will survive of us is love.
from "Ghosting" by Jennifer Erdal

The Owl

You say 'I'm exhausted'.
> **God says 'Wait on me. I will renew your strength'**
> **(Isaiah 40v31)**

You say 'I can't go on'.
> **God says 'My grace is sufficient for you'**
> **(Cor 12v9)**

You say 'I can't handle this'.
> **God says 'Give it to me. I will carry it for you'**
> **(Psalm 55v22)**

You say 'I don't know what to do'.
> **God says 'I will direct you'**
> **(Proverbs 3v6)**

You say 'I'm afraid'.
> **God says 'I didn't give you a spirit of fear**
> **but of power'**
> **(2Tim 1v7)**

You say 'I'm not sure that God means me'
> **God says 'I have loved you with an**
> **everlasting love'**
> **(Jeremiah 31v3)**
> **'Come unto me, all you who labour and are**
> **heavy laden and You will find rest for your soul'**

St Matthew 11 v 28 & 29

-~-

Your life lies before you like a path
of driven snow, be careful how you tread it
because every mark will show.

Trust Him

Trust Him when dark doubts attack you.
Trust Him when your strength is small.
Trust Him when to simply trust Him is the hardest thing of all.
Trust Him, He is ever faithful.
Trust Him, for His will is best.
Trust Him for the heart of Jesus is the only place to rest.
Trust Him, then, through doubts and sunshine.
All your cares upon Him cast
Till the storm of life is over
And your trusting days are past. *anon.*

**There may come a time in your life when you realise
that if you stand still, you will remain at this point forever.
You find that if you fall and stay down, life will pass you by.
The past has gone, and is now only a brief reflection.
The future is yet to be realised. Today is here.
Take one step at a time, with courage, faith and determination.
In time your steps will become firm and solid again.**
Victoria Forbes

They shall awake as Jacob did, and say as Jacob said, surely the
Lord is in this place, and this is no other but the House of God
and the Gate of Heaven, and into that gate they shall enter, and
in that house they shall dwell, where there shall be no cloud nor
sun, no darkness nor dazzling, but one equal light: no noise nor
silence, but one equal music; no fears nor hopes, but one equal
possession; no friends nor foes, but one equal community and
identity; no ends nor beginnings but one equal eternity.
John Donne

The Owl

An extract from 'Dew on the Grass'
by Eiluned Lewis

We who were born in Country places
Far from cities and shifting faces,
We have a birthright no man can sell
And a secret joy no man can tell.

For we are kindred to lordly things,
Orion's sword and the white owl's wings
To hawk and salmon, to bull and horse,
The wild duck's flight and the smell of gorse.

Pride of trees, swiftness of streams,
Magic of frost have shaped our dreams.
No baser vision their spirit fills
Who walk by right on the naked hills.

You cannot prevent the birds of sadness from flying over our head, but you can prevent them building nest in your hair

Chinese proverb

Meditations
by Marcus Aurelius Antoninus

Time is sort of a river of passing events, and strong is its current;
No sooner is a thing brought to sight than it is swept by and another takes
its place, And this too will be swept away.

Yesterday
is but a dream,
tomorrow a vision,
But today well lived,
makes every yesterday
a dream of happiness;
and every tomorrow
a vision of hope.
Look well, therefore,
to this day.

We grow by dreams. All big men are dreamers. They see things in the soft haze of a spring day or in the red fire of a long winter's evening. Some of us let these great dreams die, but others nourish and protect them, nurse them through bad days till they bring them to the sunshine and light which come always to those who sincerely hope that their dreams will come true. *Woodrow Wilson*

The Sandpiper

for spirit

··

Don't walk in front of me,
I may not follow.
Don't walk behind me,
I may not lead.
Walk beside me and be my friend.
Albert Camus French philosopher (1913 -1960)

The Sandpiper

Sandpiper *by Celia Thaxter (1872)*

Across the narrow beach we flit,
　　One little sandpiper and I,
And fast I gather, bit by bit,
　　The scattered driftwood bleached and dry.
The wild waves reach their hands for it,
　　The wild wind raves, the tide runs high,
As up and down the beach we flit,
　　One little sandpiper and I.

Above our heads the sullen clouds
　　Scud black and swift across the sky;
Like silent ghosts in misty shrouds
　　Stand out the white lighthouses high.
Almost as far as eye can reach
　　I see the close-reefed vessels fly,
As fast we flit along the beach,
　　One little sandpiper and I.

I watch him as he skims along,
　　Uttering his sweet and mournful cry.
He starts not at my fitful song,
　　Nor flash of fluttering drapery.
He has no thought of any wrong;
　　He scans me with a fearless eye:
Staunch friends are we, well tried and strong,
　　The little sandpiper and I.

Comrade, where wilt thou be tonight,
　　When the loosed storm breaks furiously?
My driftwood fire will burn so bright!
　　To what warm shelter canst thou fly?
I do not fear for thee, though wroth
　　The tempest rushes through the sky:
For are we not God's children both,
　　Thou, little sandpiper, and I?

Moorland Song *from Kingfisher Days by Mary Sheepshanks*

Wind in the heather sings me a song
of mountains and moorland where freedom is strong
- where mist round the fir-trees drapes curtains of sleep
and tear-stained with water, rock-faces weep.

> **Breeze in the bracken murmurs a rhyme**
> **of city-free spaces un-cloistered as time**
> **while chimes from the harebells wild honey-bees ring,**
> **and crooning and droning, a cradle-song sing.**

Pipits are piping: they flute me a chant
of cloud patterned hill tops with sunlight aslant
on weathered grey boulders where lichens have grown
a rusty green tracery printed on stone.

> **The wind and the wildness tell me a tale**
> **to heal me and help me if courage should fail:**
> **oh blessing of beauty - my heart must belong**
> **where wind through the heather blows me a song.**

• • •

From a Father to his Children

'Walk with me. Share the happiness I now have. I am in a land where
the sun warms but does not burn, where the rains sprinkle the earth with
small sweet drops and the snowflakes fall gently, not driven by the wind.
There is music and laughter and joy. Sadness and pain are gone for ever.
Only peace remains.

As we walk, I shall be with you, watching over you, cheering you on in all
that you do. I shall love you and care for you for ever as I always have done.
So love life, live it to the full for I shall be there, laughing with you, just as I
did yesterday. *anon.*

Self importance

Sometime when you're feeling important
Sometime when your ego's in bloom
Sometime when you take it for granted,
You're the best qualified in the room.

Sometime that you feel that your going
would leave an unfilled hole,
Just follow these simple instructions,
And see how they humble your soul.

Take a bucket and fill it with water,
Put your hand in it, up to your wrist
Pull it out and the hole that's remaining
Is a measure of how you'll be missed.

You can splash all you wish when you enter,
You may stir up the water galore,
But stop, and you'll find that in no time.
It looks like the same as before.

The moral in this quaint example
Is do just the best you can,
Be proud of yourself, but remember –
There's no indispensable quality man.

• • •

You are only here for a short visit.
Don't hurry. Don't worry.
And be sure to smell the flowers along the way.

Walter C Hagen (1892-1969)

A Country Walk *by Dr Taylor*

Following a diagnosis of cancer Dr Taylor started writing poetry in order to express the way he was feeling. He died in 1996.

Let me take you by the hand,
For I have much to show.
A green, a very pleasant land,
Where you and I can go.

Wander through the woods with me,
The future measured hours.
Wander free, don't count the time,
Just cast your eye on ours.

I feel the sun and love the rain
The snow and ice and gales,
Keep walking on, there's much to face,
But this spirit never fails.

A country walk, just see the scene,
Just smell and feel and hear.
Let us go and explore no more,
Be happy, lose that fear.

Cuddled in the arms as Nature's child,
Her bond human life secures.
I go, I search, and always find,
That I am only yours.

When walking through that distant wood,
Or walking through the sand.
Every step will leave my love,
On this my native land.

I have enjoyed my country walk,
A time to walk and think, and speak.
A time to look and think again,
To look inside and seek.

A Smile

A smile costs nothing, but gives much.
It takes but a moment, but the memory of it usually lasts forever.
None are so rich that can get along without it
And none are so poor but that can be made rich by it.

It enriches those who receive, without making poor those who give.
It creates sunshine in the home,
Fosters good will in business,
And is the best antidote for trouble –
And yet it cannot be begged, borrowed, or stolen, for it is of no value
Unless it is given away.

Some people are too busy to give you a smile.
Give them one of yours
For the good Lord knows that no one needs a smile so badly
As he or she who has no more smiles left to give.
Sent by Anne Pelham Burn - Aboyne

A thing of beauty is a joy for ever:
Its loveliness increases; it will never
Pass into nothingness; but still will keep
A bower quiet for us, and a sleep
Full of sweet dreams, and health, and quiet breathing.

from John Keats' epic poem, Endymion, 1818

• • •

A long line is like a long prayer;
it will never be answered.

Tweed Ghillie

To laugh often and much; to win the respect of intelligent people and the affection of children; to earn the appreciation of honest critics and endure the betrayal of false friends; to appreciate beauty; to leave the world a bit better whether by a healthy child, a garden patch or a redeemed social condition; to know even one life has breathed easier because you have lived. This is to have succeeded.

•••

Four-Feet *by Rudyard Kipling*

I have done mostly what most men do,
And pushed it out of my mind;
But I can't forget, if I wanted to,
Four-Feet trotting behind.

Day after day, the whole day through –
Wherever my road inclined –
Four-feet said, 'I am coming with you!'
And trotted along behind.

Now I must go by some other round, –
Which I shall never find –
Somewhere that does not carry the sound
Of Four-Feet trotting behind.

•••

No Charge for Love *anon.*

A farmer had some puppies he needed to sell. He painted a sign advertising the four pups and set about nailing it to a post on the edge of his yard. As he was driving the last nail into the post, he felt a tug on his overalls. He looked down into the eyes of a little boy. 'Mister,' he said, 'I want to buy one of your puppies.'

'Well,' said the farmer, as he rubbed the sweat of the back of his neck, 'These puppies come from fine parents and cost a good deal of money.' The boy dropped his head for a moment, then reaching deep into his pocket, he pulled out a handful of change and held it up to the farmer. 'I've got thirty-nine pence. Is that enough to take a look?'

'Sure,' said the farmer, and with that he let out a whistle. 'Here, Dolly!' he called. Out from the doghouse and down the ramp ran Dolly, followed by four little balls of fur. The little boy pressed his face against the chain link fence. His eyes danced with delight. As the dogs made their way to the fence, the little boy noticed something else stirring inside the doghouse. Slowly another little ball appeared, this one noticeably smaller. Down the ramp it slid. Then in a somewhat awkward manner, the little pup began hobbling toward the others, doing its best to catch up... 'I want that one,' the little boy said, pointing to the runt.

The farmer knelt down at the boy's side and said, 'Son, you don't want that puppy. He will never be able to run and play with you like these other dogs would. With that the little boy stepped back from the fence, reached down, and began rolling up one leg of his trousers. In doing so he revealed a steel brace running down both sides of his leg attaching itself to a specially made shoe. Looking back up at the farmer, he said, 'You see sir, I don't run too well myself, and he will need someone who understands.'

With tears in his eyes, the farmer reached down and picked up the little pup. Holding it carefully he handed it to the little boy. 'How much?' asked the little boy.

'No charge,' answered the farmer, 'There's no charge for love.'

• • •

I found God in the morning.
We just sat and talked.
I kept him near me
everywhere I walked.
I called God at noontime,
a heart filled with despair.
I felt his quiet presence,
I knew He was there.
We met again at sunset,
The waning of the day,
I had made him happy,
I had lived his way.
Then at bedtime I knelt
Silently in prayer.
Again his gentle presence I felt:
'Someone does care'. *anon.*

The Sandpiper

Self Harm *by Karen Downie (someone who self harms)*

An accidental short sleeve
and a lingering look.
I was shocked at the lack
of convincing it took.
'I just caught my arm
on a fence, or the door'.
You never noticed my eyes
fixed on the floor.

I always wanted to tell you
did not know where to start
to tell you my world was falling apart.
If I had the words
to cry out, I would try
but even seeing my eyes
you were ready to cry.

To hear the truth
I know it would kill you.
Understand that I'm
not doing this for me.
It's all to protect you.

The term 'self harm' is used to describe a range of things
that people do to themselves in a deliberate manner with the
intent of gaining some form emotional release. It is often
done in secret and kept hidden from other people.
Some people self-harm because they don't know how else to
cope with their emotions and pressures in their lives. Extreme
feelings such as fear, anger, guilt, shame, helplessness, self-
hatred, unhappiness, depression or despair can build up over
time and when these feelings become unbearable, self-harm
can be a way of dealing with them. 'Pain on the outside is
so much easier to deal with than pain on the inside'.

'Mr. God, this is Anna.'
by Fynn

...After the evening meal was finished and all the bits and pieces put away, Anna and I would settle down to some activity, generally of her choosing. Fairy stories were dismissed as mere pretend stories; living was real and living was interesting, and by and large, fun. Reading the Bible wasn't a great success. She tended to regard it as a primer, strictly for the infants... Religion was for doing things, not for reading about doing things. Once you had got the message there wasn't much point in going over and over the same old ground. Our local parson was taken aback when he asked her about God. The conversation went as follows:

'Do you believe in God?'
'Yes.'
'Do you know what God is?'
'Yes.'
'What is God then?'
'He's God!'
'Do you go to church?'
'No.'
'Why not?'
'Because I know it all!'
'What do you know?'
'I know to love Mister God and to love people and cats and dogs and spiders and flowers and trees' and the catalog went on 'with all of me.'

Anna had by-passed all the non-essentials and distilled centuries of learning into one sentence: 'And God said love me, love them, and love it, and don't forget to love yourself.'

The Sandpiper

Many Winters *by Nancy Wood*

All my life is a dance.
When I was young and feeling the earth,
My steps were quick and easy.
The beat of the earth was so loud
That my drum was silent beside it.
All of my life rolled out from my feet
Like my land which had no end as far as I could see.
The rhythm of my life was pure and free.
As I grew older my feet kept dancing so hard
That I wore a spot in the earth.
At the same time I made a hole in the sky.
I danced to the sun and the rain and the moon lifted me up
So that I could dance to the stars.
My head touched the clouds sometimes
And my feet danced deep in the earth
So that I became the music I danced to everywhere.
It was the music I dance to everywhere,
It was the music of life.
Now my steps are slow and hard
And my body fails my spirit,
Yet my dance is still within me and
My song is the air I breathe.
My song insists that I keep dancing forever.
My song insists that I keep rhythm
With all of the earth and the sky.
My song insists that I will never die.

• • •

How poor are they that have no patience!
What wound did ever heal but by degrees?

Othello - William Shakespeare(1564-1616)

Dust if you Must

'Dust if you must, but wouldn't it be better
To paint a picture or write a letter,
Bake a cake or plant a seed.
Ponder the difference between want and need.

Dust if you must, but there's not much time,
With rivers to swim and mountains to climb,
Music to hear and books to read,
Friends to cherish and life to lead.

Dust if you must, but the world's out there,
With the sun in your eyes, the wind in your hair,
A flutter of snow, a shower of rain.
This day will not come around again.

Dust if you must, but bear in mind,
Old age will come and it's not kind.
And when you go and go you must,
You, yourself, will make more dust.' *anon.*

• • •

The Difference

I got up early one morning and rushed right into the day;
I had so much to accomplish and I didn't have time to pray.
Problems just tumbled about me and heavier came each task.
'Why doesn't God help me?' I wondered. He answered, 'You didn't ask'.
I wanted to see joy and beauty but the day toiled on, gray and bleak,
I wondered why God didn't show me. He said, 'But you didn't seek'.
I tried to come into God's presence; I used all my keys at the lock.
God gently and lovingly chided, 'My child, you didn't knock'.
I woke up early this morning and paused before entering the day.
I had so much to accomplish and I had to take time to pray. *anon.*

Don't label me *by Karen Downie (someone who self harms)*

Don't put me in a box
Or label me
I'm just trying to be myself
So please just let me be.

**I'm not an emo
Just because I cut
When I dress up
Don't call me a slut
I'm not frigid
When I don't want sex
Nor am I ignorant
When I don't answer texts.**

When I'm quiet
It doesn't mean I'm meek
If I look a little different
Don't call me a freak
If I am clever
I'm not always a swot
My head's not in the clouds
If I think an awful lot.

**I'm not a psycho
If I freak out
Nor when I am drunk
Do I become a lout
I'm not weak
Just because I cry
Don't class me as a failure
If I gave it my best try.**

Labelling only
causes trouble
Who wants to be placed
in their own little bubble?
I don't want to be judged
Just for being me
I will live my life
Being me, I am free.

Halfway down the stairs

Halfway down the stairs
Is a stair where I sit:
There isn't any other stair quite like it.
I'm not at the bottom,
I'm not at the top:
So this is the stair where I always stop.
Halfway up the stairs
Isn't up, and isn't down.
It isn't in the nursery, it isn't in the town:
And all sorts of funny thoughts
Run round my head:
'It isn't really anywhere! It's somewhere else instead!'

A.A. Milne from When We Were Very Young

• • •

A Child is like a butterfly in the wind
Some can fly higher than others,
But each one flies the best it can.
Why compare one against the other?
Each one is different.
Each one is special.
Each one is beautiful.

• • •

Horses she loved, laughter and the sun,
All beauty, wide spaces and the open air,
The trust of all dumb living things she won.
And never knew the luck too good to share.

And though she may not ride this way again,
Her joyous spirit rides onward yet,
Freed from all chance of weariness or pain,
Forbidding us to mourn or forget.

Patricia Mitchell

The Sandpiper

Break, break, break *by Lord Alfred Tennyson (1809-1892)*

Break, break, break
On thy cold grey stones, O Sea!
And I would that my tongue could utter
The thoughts that arise in me.

> **O well for the fisherman's boy,**
> **That he shouts with his sister at play!**
> **O well for the sailor lad,**
> **That he sings in his boat on the bay!**

And the stately ships go on
To their haven under the hill;
But O for the touch of a vanished hand,
And the sound of a voice that is still!

> **Break, break, break**
> **At the foot of thy crags, O Sea!**
> **But the tender grace of a day that is dead**
> **Will never come back to me.**

• • •

Far From The Madding Crowd *by Nixon Waterman*

It seems to me I'd like to go
Where bells don't ring, nor whistles blow,
Nor clocks don't strike, nor gongs sound,
And I'd have stillness all around.
Not real stillness, but just the trees,
Low whispering, or the hum of bees,
Or brooks faint babbling over stones,
In strangely, softly tangled tones.
Or maybe a cricket or katydid,
Or the songs of birds in the hedges hid,
Or just some such sweet sound as these,
To fill a tired heart with ease.

As you slide down the banisters of life may the splinters always point in the right direction...

Irish toast

The Sandpiper

Trout Fishing *by Eunice Lamberton 1873*

Give me a rod of the split bamboo,
a rainy day and a fly or two,
a mountain stream where the eddies play,
and mists hang low o'er the winding way,

Give me a haunt by the furling brook,
A hidden spot in a mossy nook,
No sound save hum of the drowsy bee,
or lone bird's tap on the hollow tree.

The world may roll with its busy throng,
And phantom scenes on its way along,
Its stocks may rise, or its stocks may fall,
Ah! What care I for its baubles all?

I cast my fly o'er the troubled rill,
Luring the beauties by magic skill,
With mind at rest and a heart at ease,
And drink delight at the balmy breeze.

A lusty trout to my glad surprise,
Speckled and bright on the crest arise,
Then splash and plunge in a dazzling whirl,
Hope springs anew as the wavelets curl.

Gracefully swinging from left to right,
Action so gentle - motion so slight,.
Tempting, enticing, on craft intent,
Till yielding tip by the game is bent.

Drawing in slowly, then letting go
Under the ripples where mosses grow
Doubting my fortune, lost in a dream,
Blessing the land of forest and stream.

• • •

As pants the heart for cooling streams
when heated in the chase,
So longs my flask my souls for thee
And thy refreshing taste.

O for a Royal, a thumping Royal
my telescope doth yearn.
O when shall I, in Viniglen,
His sweeping tines discern?

Shake not my hand,
Race not my heart,
Crawl on beyond the brow,
To where he waits and beckons you,
And whispers 'Take him now'.

Boreland version of Hymn No 238

• • •

Kids who are different *by Digby Wolfe*

Here's to the kids who are different
The kids who don't always get As.
The kids who have ears twice the size of their peers,
And noses that go on for day...
Here's to the kids who are different,
The kids they call crazy or dumb,
The kids who don't fit ,
with the guts and the grit,
Who dance to the beat of a different drum.
Here's to the kids who are different,
The kids with the mischievous streak,
For when they have grown,
as history's shown,
It's their difference that makes them unique.

• • •

Getting Better at Goodbye *by Michael J. Rosen (with thanks)*

Goodbyes are harder than hello,
at least for me to say.
And though I'm better at goodbye,
I'd always rather stay.

Just what's so good about goodbye?
It always comes too soon,
and then it always stays too long.
Goodbye's a boring tune.

It used to be when Mummy left,
I cried till she returned…
and then I'd miss the babysitter!
Goodbye is hard to learn.

Or when my Dad drove me to school,
I wouldn't leave his side.
'You're a big boy now,' he'd say.
'Oh no, I'm not,' I lied.

I'm practising goodbyes. It helps:
goodbye to outgrown coats,
to cowboy boots that just don't fit,
goodbye to swimming floats.

We sold the house where I was born,
my yard, my climbing tree,
and all the secrets my room kept
for no one else but me.

But I've been glad to say to goodbye
to car seats, strollers, bibs,
to training wheels and baby teeth
and bubble baths and cribs.

The puppies that our boxer had
I knew we couldn't keep.
One by one, we found them homes.
Each goodbye made me weep.

You know, I didn't mind goodbye
when Joey next door moved.
He always started fights with me,
so now things have improved.

When Gram and Grampa visit us,
they only stay a week,
but after seven days with them
goodbye is hard to speak.

Maybe goodbye is like the sun:
it sets before my eyes,
and leaves me in the darkness so…
hello's a big surprise!

Goodbye to summer, summer camp,
to shorts I just unpacked.
And soon, it's goodbye autumn leaves,
that wave their colours back.

I wanted to, but didn't keep,
a toad that I had caught.
It wanted to be free, whether
I said goodbye or not.

But last year when my great aunt died,
– she'd just turned ninety-five –
we couldn't say goodbye to her
as though she were alive.

I saw some grown-ups – old men, too –
wiping their tears away.
I guess goodbye may always be
much harder on some days.

Goodbye is just the early part
of some future hello.
It's not an ending,
it's a start of something you don't know.

The Sandpiper

Flight *by Brian Young*

How can they know that joy to be alive
Who have not flown?
To loop and spin and roll and climb and dive,
The very sky one's own.
The urge of power while engines race,
The sting of speed,
The rude winds' buffet on one's face,
To live indeed.
How can they know the grandeur of the sky,
The earth below,
The restless sea, and waves that break and die
With ceaseless ebb and flow;
The morning sun on drifting clouds
And rolling downs–
And valley mist that shrouds
The chimneyed towns?
So long has puny man to earth been chained
Who now is free,
And with the conquest of the air has gained
A glorious liberty.
How splendid is this gift He gave
On high to roam,
The sun a friend, the earth a slave,
The heavens home...

• • •

Calm me O Lord as you stilled the storm.
Still me O Lord, keep me from harm.
Let all the tumult within me cease.
Enfold me Lord within your peace. *anon.*

Life is not measured by the number of breaths we take, but by the moments that take our breath away.

The Sandpiper

Time is Short

Have you ever watched kids
On a merry-go-round?
Or listened to the rain
Slapping on the ground?
Ever followed a butterfly's erratic flight?
Or gazed at the sun into the fading night?

You'd better slow down
Don't dance so fast.
Time is short.
The music won't last.

Do you run through each day
On the fly?
When you ask 'How are you?'
Do you hear the reply?
When the day is done
Do you lie in your bed
With the next hundred chores
Running through your head?

You'd better slow down
Don't dance so fast.
Time is short.
The music won't last.

Ever told your child,
We'll do it tomorrow?
And in your haste,
Not see his sorrow?
Ever lost touch,
Let a good friendship die
Cause you never had time
To call and say 'Hi'?

You'd better slow down
Don't dance so fast.
Time is short.
The music won't last.

When you run so fast to get somewhere
You miss half the fun of getting there.
When you worry and hurry through your day,
It is like an unopened gift....
Thrown away.
Life is not a race.
Do take it slower
Hear the music
Before the song is over.
anon.

• • •

*Humour is the great thing,
the saving thing. The minute it
crops up, all our irritations and
resentments slip away and a
sunny spirit takes their place.*

Mark Twain (1835-1910)

Migration
from Dancing Blues to Skylarks Mary Sheepshanks

High on my windswept hill
I live beneath a flight path.

Each year I thrill
to hear the whispering wings
and haunting fog-horn cry
before I see ship's anchors tossed
across the ripples of an ocean sky.

Strong pinions beat and stretch
to shift the air and race
the striptease act of autumn trees;

their rhythmic music sings
of hedgerow berries' juicy yield
and hawthorn skies at dusk;
first frosts on stubble fields
a search for winter food;
flick-knives concealed
inside the pockets of
a gangster breeze.

Evenings grow dark again
and summer's dead

– but
the wild geese are back
and sailing overhead.

• • •

A Gaelic Farewell

May the road rise up to meet you
May the wind always be at your back
May the sun shine warm upon your face
the rains fall soft upon your fields
and until we meet again
May God hold you in the palm of His Hand *anon.*

• • •

He Wishes For The Cloths Of Heaven *by William Butler Yeats*

Had I the heavens' embroidered cloths,
Enwrought with golden and silver light,
The blue and the dim and the dark cloths
Of night and light and the half-light,
I would spread the cloths under your feet:
But I, being poor, have only my dreams;
I have spread my dreams under your feet;
Tread softly because you tread on my dreams.

• • •

'I Have Earache'

2000 BC	Here, eat this root.
AD 1000	That root is heathen. Here, say this prayer.
AD 1850	Prayer is superstition. Here, drink this potion
AD 1940	That potion is snake oil. Here, swallow this pill.
AD 1985	That pill is ineffective. Here, take this antibiotic.
AD 2000	That antibiotic is ineffective. Here, eat this root.

anon.

• • •

The Sandpiper

Have you ever been in love?

Have you ever been in love? Horrible isn't it? It makes you so vulnerable. It opens your chest and it opens up your heart and it means that someone can get inside you and mess you up. You build up all these defences, you build up a whole suit of armour, so that nothing can hurt you, then one stupid person, no different from any other stupid person, wanders into your stupid life... You give them a piece of you. They didn't ask for it. They did something dumb one day, like kiss you or smile at you, and then your life isn't your own anymore. Love takes hostages. It gets inside you. It eats you out and leaves you crying in the darkness, so simple a phrase like 'maybe we should be just friends' turns into a glass splinter working its way into your heart. It hurts. Not just in the imagination. Not just in the mind. It's a soul-hurt, a real gets-inside-you-and-rips-you-apart pain. I hate love.

Neil Gaiman

•••

'Happiness is like a butterfly, the more you chase it, the more it will elude you. But if you turn your attention to other things, it comes and softly sits on your shoulder.'

by Nathanial Hawthorne

Friends in Paradise *by Henry Vaughan*

He that hath found some fledged bird's nest, may know
    At first sight, if the bird be flown;
But what fair well or grove he sings in now,
    That is to him unknown.

And yet as Angels in some brighter dreams
    Call to the soul, when man doth sleep:
So some strange thoughts transcend our wonted themes
    And into glory peep.

• • •

I believe in all things beautiful the beauty of simple things.

I believe in music where melody is quickly found,

and in poems that sound like song.

I believe in books that hold no ugly thought, in pictures that

rest the eye and soothe the senses, and in plays that keep the heart young.

Little things delight me: a sunbeam on a blade of grass;

a dewdrop in the heart of a flower; a daisy with a rosy frill

I believe in joy and quick laughter in sentiment,

in love, in reverence.

I believe in all things beautiful

I believe in God   M. Aumônier

Teamwork

I
read
about
the reason
migrating geese
fly in a V-formation.
Each goose flapping its
wings creates an upward
lift for the goose that follows. When all the geese do
their part, the whole flock has
a 71% greater flying range than if
each bird were to fly alone. Also when
a goose begins to lag behind, the others
'honk' it into position. The teamwork appli-
cations here are tremendous. I am sure it is at
least 71% easier to work the teamwork way flying
in the flock than trying it alone, and it is good to
have the advantage of being moved back into position if
we stray from our goals.
That's what teamwork is all about!

• • •

Heaven is where the police are British,
the chefs French, the lovers Italian,
the mechanics German,
and all organised by the Swiss.

Hell is where the police are German,
the chefs British, the lovers Swiss,
the mechanics French,
and all organised by the Italians

• • •

Sea-Fever *by John Masefield (1878-1967)*

I must go down to the seas again, to the lonely sea and the sky,
And all I ask is a tall ship and a star to steer her by;
And the wheel's kick and the wind's song and the white sail's shaking,
And a gray mist on the sea's face, and a gray dawn breaking.

I must go down to the seas again, for the call of the running tide
Is a wild call and a clear call that may not be denied;
And all I ask is a windy day with the white clouds flying,
And the flung spray and the blown spume, and the sea-gulls crying.

I must go down to the seas again, to the vagrant gypsy life,
To the gull's way and the whale's way, where the wind's like a whetted knife;
And all I ask is a merry yarn from a laughing fellow-rover,
And quiet sleep and a sweet dream when the long trick's over.

• • •

The Sandpiper

The Doctor's Dilemma *from Thinning Grapes by Mary Sheepshanks*

I specialise in lupins
They're my pride and my delight
I fertilise and water them,
Converse with them each night;
They win me many prizes
They're the glory of my life
When I show them to my neighbours
And share them with my wife.

I look at all this beauty
That God and I have made
(I buy the seed, He made the earth,
I dig it with my spade)
And when I dwell with pleasure
On our joint co-operation
I look upon my flower-beds
With awful consternation:
For my very special lupins
In the bed which I have dug
Have been absolutely ruined
By a hungry burgling slug.

I've always felt that there is room
On earth for one and all
To live in perfect harmony
Along with Dr Hall
So I tell the slugs I love them
And I also tell them firmly
That the flowers are solely mine!
I go to bed quite happy,
Feel I dealt well with this matter
But next day my lupins look much worse
And the slugs are even fatter.

I pile the slugs in flower-pots
And take them far away
And instruct them, very kindly,
That this is where they stay.
I know that I have treated them
As fairly as I could
But slugs are very greedy,
And the taste of lupin, good:
The minute that I leave them
They require a tasty snack
And by the time I'm home again,
The slugs are also back.

This time I am very angry,
To a Garden Centre drive
And intend that pretty shortly
There will be no slugs alive:
I say I wish to purchase
A really lethal pellet
And the Garden Centre stock one
And are very keen to sell it.
Now I spend my days in healing
And cure the sick and ill
But suddenly I wonder
If a doctor ought to kill?

I see those lovely lupins
In the bed which I have dug
But question: are they meant for me
Or are they for the slug?
I ponder on the matter
Of God's manifold creation
And decide perhaps the slugs and I
Should go to Arbitration

The Sandpiper

I thank you God for most this amazing day *by E.E.Cummings*

I thank you God for most this amazing
day: for the leaping greenly spirits of trees
and a blue true dream of sky;and for everything
which is natural which is infinite which is yes

(I who have died am alive again today,
and this is the sun's birthday; this is the birth
day of life and of love and wings: and of the gay
great happening illimitably earth)

how should tasting touching hearing seeing
breathing any – lifted from the no
of all nothing – human merely being
doubt unimaginable You?

(now the ears of my ears awake and
now the eyes of my eyes are opened)

• ● •

I laugh,
I love,
I hope,
I try,
I hurt,
I need,
I fear,
I cry.

And I know you do the same things too, so we're
really not that different, me and you.

Colin Raye

I thought of you with love today but that is nothing new,

I thought about you yesterday and days before that too.

I think of you in silence, I often speak your name.

All I have are memories and your picture in a frame.

Your memory is my keepsake with which I'll never part.

God has you in His keeping; I have you in my heart.

anon

• • •

Que sera sera

Whatever will be, will be

• • •

The Seagull
I watched a seagull spread its wings to rise into the blue.
Out toward the far horizon, straight and strong it flew,
But slowly it became a speck and disappeared from sight,
Vanishing behind a hazy veil of golden light.
Lost to view, but still it flew, though not observed by me.
So it is when souls go out in to eternity.
They pass beyond the range of vision and
We say they've gone,
But like the bird that fades into the distance, they go on
On to a greater life the journey to complete
Across the veiled dividing line where earth
And heaven meet. *anon*

The Sandpiper

I Wandered Lonely as a Cloud *by William Wordsworth (1770-1850)*

I wandered lonely as a cloud
That floats on high o'er vales and hills,
When all at once I saw a crowd,
A host, of golden daffodils;
Beside the lake, beneath the trees,
Fluttering and dancing in the breeze.

Continuous as the stars that shine
And twinkle on the milky way,
They stretched in never-ending line
Along the margin of a bay:
Ten thousand saw I at a glance,
Tossing their heads in sprightly dance.

The waves beside them danced; but they
Out-did the sparkling waves in glee:–
A Poet could not but be gay
In such a jocund company:
I gazed and gazed but little thought
What wealth the show to me had brought:

For oft when on my couch I lie
In vacant or in pensive mood,
They flash upon that inward eye
Which is the bliss of solitude,
And then my heart with pleasure fills,
And dances with the Daffodils.

• • •

*'If at times things look glum,
Rest assured there's worst to come!'*

LOON – Alasdair Hilleary

from Jock of the Bushveld *by Sir Percy Fitzpatrick (1862 -1931)*

I was lying on my side chewing a grass stem, and Jock lay down in front of me a couple of feet away. It was a habit of his: he liked to watch my face, and often when I rolled over to ease one side and lie on the other, he would get up when he found my back turned to him and come round deliberately to the other side and sling himself down in front of me again. There he would lie with his hind legs sprawled on one side, his front legs straight out, and his head resting on his paws. He would lie like that without a move, his little dark eyes fixed on mine. In the loneliness of that evening I looked into his steadfast resolute face with its darker muzzle and bright faithful eyes that looked so soft and brown when there was nothing to do but got so beady black when it came to fighting. I felt very friendly to the comrade who was little more than a puppy still; and he seemed to feel something too; for as I lay there chewing the straw and looking at him, he stirred his stump of a tail in the dust an inch or so from time-to-time to let me know that he undertood all about it and that it was all right as long as we were together.

• • •

The Lie of the Grass
from Dancing Blues to Skylark by Mary Sheepshanks

Love is like
the strongest wind
the softest breeze
which in their passing
leaves memories
in the lie of the grass

So may the imprint
of your love
stay on the meadow
of my life

for ever.

If a Dog Were Your Teacher!

You would learn stuff like...

- When loved ones come home, always run to greet them.
- Never pass up the opportunity to go for a joyride.
- Allow the experience of fresh air and the wind in your face to be pure ecstasy.
- When it's in your best interest, practise obedience.
- Let others know when they've invaded your territory.
- Take naps and stretch before rising.
- Run, romp, and play daily.
- Thrive on attention and let people touch you.
- Avoid biting, when a simple growl will do.
- On warm days, stop to lie on your back on the grass.
- On hot days, drink lots of water and lie under a shady tree.
- When you're happy, dance around and wag your entire body.
- No matter how often you're scolded, don't buy into the guilt thing and pout – run right back and make friends.
- Delight in the simple joy of a long walk.
- Eat with gusto and enthusiasm. Stop when you have had enough.
- Be loyal.
- Never pretend to be something you're not.
- If what you want lies buried, dig until you find it. And MOST of all...
- When someone is having a bad day, be silent, sit close by and offer a gentle nuzzle.

anon.

• • •

Let your life lightly dance on the edges of time like dew on the tip of a leaf.

anon.

I Said a Prayer

I said a prayer for you today
And know God must have heard,
I felt the answer in my heart
Although he spoke no word.
I didn't ask for wealth or fame,
I knew you wouldn't mind.
I asked him for some treasures
Of a far more lasting kind.
I asked that he'd be near you
At the start of each new day,
To grant you health and blessings
And friends to share the way.
I asked for happiness for you
In all things great and small.
But it was for his loving care
I prayed for most of all. *anon.*

• • •

The wise words that your mother said
And you pretended not to hear,
May linger somewhere in your head
And return in later years.
Her sound advice from long ago
Could well be what you need
To help you know and they may show
The best way to proceed.

Prayer for a Grandchild

Let no-one hurry him Lord.
Give him the rare, the incomparable gift of time.
Days to dream, dragonfly days, days when the kingfisher
Suddenly opens for him a window on wonder.
Let no-one chivvy him Lord; let him meander
Lark-happy through childhood, by fern bordered streams
Fringed butter-yellow with king cups; by secret ways
That paws have worn through the wild;
Give him cuckoo-land days and owl's cry
By night.

Dear Lord, give him rainbows:
Show him a nest filled with sky-blue promises;
Scoop up the sounding oceans for him in a shell.
Let him keep his dreams
So that he will always turn his face to the light:
Live merrily, love well;
Hold out ungloved hands to flower and child;
Be easy with animals; come to terms with time
Lord let him keep his dreams;
Let his riches be remembered happy days. *anon.*

• • •

My Big Toe *by Michael Leunig*

My big toe is an honest man
So down to earth and normal
Always true unto himself
And pleasantly informal
Full of simple energy
Contented with his role
If all of me was more like him
I'd be a happy soul

When at heart you should be sad
Pondering the joys we had
Listen and keep very still
If the lowing from the hill
Or the tolling of a bell
Do not serve to break the spell
Listen, you may be allowed
To hear my laughter from a cloud

• • •

66 Look to this day, for it is Life,
The very life of Life.
In its brief course
lie all the realities of existence,
The joy of growth,
The splendour of action,
The glory of power.
For yesterday is but a memory
And tomorrow is only a vision.
But today well lived
makes every yesterday
a memory of happiness.
And every tomorrow
a vision of hope.
Look well, therefore, to this day 99
Ancient Sanskrit poem

The Sandpiper

It seems so hard to understand...

It seems so hard to understand
As I look out across the land
That all I view belongs to me,
I ought to take more time to see!

The distant hills and mountains high,
The rolling clouds and bright blue sky,
No one can take these views from me
As long as I have eyes to see!

The song of birds so gay and clear
That fill the morning air with cheer
And fragrant flowers of every hue
That stand erect bedecked with dew,
All these and more belong to me
If I but use my eyes to see.

When evening shadows gather nigh
And twinkling stars light up the sky
I hear my master say to me
'I made it all for you to see'
My heart grows warm with faith and pride
To know that He is by my side. *anon.*

• • •

It is a lovely day tomorrow,
tomorrow is a lovely day;
come and feast your tear dimmed eyes
on tomorrow's clear blue skies.

If today your heart is weary,
if every little thing looks grey,
Just forget your sorrows and learn to say,
Tomorrow is a lovely day. *anon.*

Keep Calm and Carry On

• • •

O God, we praise thee for the arching sky and the blessed winds,
for the driving clouds and the stars on high,
for the trees and for the grass under our feet.
We thank thee for our senses by which we can see
the splendour of the morning and hear the happy song of birds,
and smell the breath of spring.
Grant us, we pray, hearts wide open to all this joy and beauty,
lest we pass heedless and unseeing when the thorn bush by the wayside
is aflame with thy glory.
Amen. *anon.*

• • •

The Sandpiper

To the Mother of a Little Girl *by Marion Doyle*

Let her laugh and dance and sing
Touch gently every lovely thing
Now while dandelions wear
The very colour of her hair
And briarcliff roses seek the delicate colour of her cheek
While the iris reach her shoulder
– all too soon she will be older

Full of wisdom, dignified
Walking slowly by your side
Now while all is mystery
Let her taste, touch, hear, and see
Let her laugh and dance and sing

Youth is such a transient thing
Soon the year will turn and then –
Grave and Pensive she'll be ten

• • •

**The more you give
the more you get
the more you laugh,
the less you fret,
the more you do unselfishly,
the more you live abundantly,
the more of everything you share
the more you'll always have to spare,
the more you love,
the more you find,
that life is good,
and friends are kind,
for only what we give away,
enriches us from day to day.**
Helen Steiner Rice 1900-1981

The Mirror *by Gillian Downie – someone with anorexia*

I look into the mirror and what do I see?
Two big blue eyes staring straight back at me
A stranger quite pretty with makeup so nice
But surely to be attractive there must be a price?
To shrink and to disappear was always my goal
So sure there were flaws deep down in my soul
I'd look in the mirror and all I would see
Were two tortured eyes staring straight back at me

I look into the mirror and what do I see?
Is it really possible this person could be me?
To be feminine was wrong, it just didn't feel right
To stay safe and childlike I put up a fight
Doing anything I could to avoid other's gaze
I passed through each day in a starvation induced haze
I'd look in the mirror and all I would see
Were flaws and imperfections that were all that made me

I look into the mirror and what do I see?
Two big blue eyes staring straight back at me
But look under the sadness and perhaps I might find
Hope and determination of quite a different kind
Where once I thought there could only be suffering and pain
I now know that from life there could be so much more to gain
I've looked in the mirror and what did I see
Was the person that I hope will one day be free

• • •

**Let your boat of life be light, packed with only what you need –
simple pleasures, one or two friends, worth the name, a dog, and a
pipe or two, enough to eat and enough to wear, and a little more
than enough to drink; for thirst is a dangerous thing.**
Jerome K. Jerome, 3 Men in a Boat

The Sandpiper

A Sandpiper to Bring You Joy *written by Mary Sherman Hilbert*

She was six years old when I first met her on the beach near where I live. I drive to this beach, a distance of three or four miles, whenever the world begins to close in on me. She was building a sand castle or something and looked up, her eyes blue as the sea.

'Hello,' she said. I answered with a nod, not really in the mood to bother with a small child.

'I'm building,' she said.

'I see that. What is it?' I asked, not caring.

'Oh I don't know, I just like the feel of the sand.'

That sounds good, I thought, and slipped off my shoes. A sandpiper glided by.

'That's a joy,' the child said.

'It's what?'

'It's a joy. My mama says sandpipers come to bring us joy.'

The bird went on down the beach. 'Good-bye, joy,' I muttered to myself, 'Hello pain,' and turned to walk on. I was depressed; my life seemed completely out of balance.

'What's your name?' She wouldn't give up.

'Ruth,' I answered. 'I'm Ruth Peterson.'

'Mine's Wendy,... and I'm six.'

'Hi, Wendy.'

She giggled. 'You're funny,' she said.

In spite of my gloom I laughed too and walked on.

Her musical giggle followed me. 'Come again, Mrs. P,' she called. 'We'll have another happy day.'

The days and weeks that followed belonged to others: a group of unruly BoyScouts, PTA meetings, an ailing mother. The sun was shining one morning as I took my hands out of the dishwater.

'I need a sandpiper,' I said to myself, gathering up my coat. The never-changing balm of the seashore awaited me. The breeze was chilly, but I strode along, trying to recapture the serenity I needed. I had forgotten the child and was startled when she appeared.

'Hello, Mrs. P,' she said. 'Do you want to play?'

'What did you have in mind?' I asked, with a twinge of annoyance.

'I don't know, you say.'

'How about charades?' I asked sarcastically.

The tinkling laughter burst forth again. 'I don't know what that is.'

'Then let's just walk.' Looking at her, I noticed the delicate fairness of her face.

'Where do you live?' I asked.

'Over there.' She pointed toward a row of summer cottages. Strange, I thought, in winter.

'Where do you go to school?'

'I don't go to school. Mommy says we're on vacation.'

She chattered little girl talk as we strolled up the beach, but my mind was on other things. When I left for home, Wendy said it had been a happy day. Feeling surprisingly better, I smiled at her and agreed.

Three weeks later, I rushed to my beach in a state of near panic. I was in no mood even to greet Wendy. I thought I saw her mother on the porch and felt like demanding she keep her child at home.

'Look, if you don't mind,' I said crossly when Wendy caught up with me, 'I'd rather be alone today.'

She seemed unusually pale and out of breath.

'Why?' she asked.

I turned on her and shouted, 'Because my mother died!'- and thought, my God, why was I saying this to a little child?

'Oh,' she said quietly, 'then this is a bad day.'

'Yes, and yesterday and the day before that and - oh, go away!'

'Did it hurt?'

'Did what hurt?' I was exasperated with her, with myself.

'When she died?'

'Of course it hurt!' I snapped, wrapped up in myself. I strode off.

A month or so after that, when I next went to the beach, she wasn't there. Feeling guilty, ashamed and admitting to myself I missed her, I went up to the cottage after my walk and knocked at the door. A drawn-looking young woman with honey-colored hair opened the door.

'Hello,' I said. 'I'm Ruth Peterson. I missed your little girl today and wondered where she was.'

'Oh yes, Mrs. Peterson, please come in.' 'Wendy talked of you so much. I'm afraid I allowed her to bother you. If she was a nuisance, please accept my apologies.'

'Not at all - she's a delightful child,' I said, suddenly realising that I meant it.
'Where is she?'

'Wendy died last week, Mrs. Peterson. She had leukemia. Maybe she didn't tell you.'

Struck dumb, I groped for a chair. My breath caught.

'She loved this beach; so when she asked to come, we couldn't say no. She seemed so much better here and had a lot of what she called 'Happy Days.' But the last few weeks, she declined rapidly...' Her voice faltered. 'She left something for you... if only I can find it. Could you wait a moment while I look?'

I nodded stupidly, my mind racing for something, anything, to say to this lovely young woman.

She handed me a smeared envelope, with **MRS. P** printed in bold, childish letters. Inside was a drawing in bright crayon hues - a yellow beach, a blue sea, a brown bird. Underneath was carefully printed:

A SANDPIPER TO BRING YOU JOY

Tears welled up in my eyes, and a heart that had almost forgotten how to love opened wide. I took Wendy's mother in my arms. 'I'm sorry, I'm sorry, I'm so sorry,' I muttered over and over, and we wept together.

The precious little picture is framed now and hangs in my study. Six words - one for each year of her life-that speak to me of inner harmony, courage, undemanding love. A gift from a child with sea-blue eyes and hair the color of sand - who taught me the gift of love.

•••

Losers make promises, winners make commitments

A Scottish Blessing

May the blessing of light be on you
- light without and light within.
May the blessed sunlight shine on you like a great peat fire,
so that stranger and friend may come and warm himself at it.
And may light shine out of the two eyes of you,
like a candle set in the window of a house,
bidding the wanderer come in out of the storm.
And may the blessing of the rain be on you,
may it beat upon your Spirit and wash it fair and clean,
and leave there a shining pool where the blue of Heaven shines,
and sometimes a star.
And may the blessing of the earth be on you,
soft under your feet as you pass along the roads,
soft under you as you lie out on it, tired at the end of day;
and may it rest easy over you when, at last, you lie out under it.
May it rest so lightly over you that your soul may be out from
under it quickly; up and off and on its way to God.
And now may the Lord bless you, and bless you kindly. Amen.

• • •

The Way of the White Clouds
by Lama Govinda

To see the greatness of a mountain one must keep one's distance.
To understand its form one must move around it.
To experience its moods one must see it at sunrise and sunset
— at noon and at midnight —
In sun and in rain
— in snow and in storm —
in summer and in winter and in all other seasons.
He who can see the mountain
like this comes near to the life of the mountain,
a life that is as intense and varied as that of a human being.

The Oyster

There once was an oyster whose story I'll tell,
Who found that some sand had worked under his shell.
Just one little grain but it gave him a pain,
For oysters have feelings that are very plain.
Now did he berate this working of fate,
That left him in such a deplorable state?
Did he curse the government, call for an election,
And say that the sea should have some protection?
Well, years passed by, as years always do,
Till he came to his destiny – oyster stew!
But the small grain of sand that bothered him so,
Was a beautiful pearl, all richly aglow.
Now this tale has a moral, for isn't it grand,
What an oyster can do with a small grain of sand?
And what couldn't we do if we'd only begin
With all of the things that get under our skin?

• • •

Prayer for our Healing *by Marjorie Pizer*

When I feel overwhelmed by destruction,
Let me go down to the sea.
Let me sit by the immeasurable ocean
And watch the surf
Beating in and running out all day and all night,
Let me sit by the sea
And have the bitter sea winds
Slap my cheeks with their cold, damp hands
Until I am sensible again.
Let me look at the sky at night
And let the stars tell me
Of limitless horizons and unknown universes
Until I am grown calm and strong once more.

'Misce stultitiam consiliis brevem: Dulce est desipere in loco'

'Mix a little foolishness with your serious plans:
it's lovely to be silly at the right moment' Horace 65-8 B.C.

The Sandpiper

Farewell Poem *by the 9th Earl of Southesk*

Oh! That I were young again
Roaming through the forest glen,
Where the solemn fir-trees sigh,
Rivers running golden by.
My youth, my youth, will none restore!
No more, no never, never more.

Oh! The dreams, the idle dreams!
Up the rocks, and o'er the streams
Where the birches balmy smell,
Heather-bloom, and foxglove-bell.
My youth, my youth will not restore!
No more, no never, never more.

Oh! The moan, the empty moan!
Calling joys for ever flown.
'Mong the quiet garden flowers
Happy halt mine evening hours-
Till youth, my youth, the Heavens restore,
Once more, for ever, ever more.

• • •

**What can we say when we consider the loss of a friend,
a colleague, a mentor? How do we express the sense of
loss, the grief, the awful longing for what might have
been? There is a way. We do it with a word, a simple
word, a word we all recognise. It is a word that enters
the lives of us all. It is a word that expresses emotions
across the whole gamut of human feelings, a word that
touches all of our loves as well as all of our griefs.
What shall we say when we consider that he has gone?
We shall say the word, and the word is ...FUCK!**

Dibbs Mather, Eulogy for Australian by Hugh Atkinson

Some Things I Have Learned

I've learned that you can get by on charm for about 15 minutes.
After that, you'd better know something.
I've learned that you shouldn't compare yourself to the best others can do,
but the best that you can do.
I've learned that it is not what you have in your life,
but WHO you have in your life that counts.
I've learned that it takes years to build up trust,
and only seconds to destroy it.
I've learned that you can do something in an instant
that will give you heartache for life.
I've learned that no matter how thin you slice it, there are always two sides.
I've learned that it is a lot easier to react than it is to think.
I've learned that you can keep going long after you think you can't.
I've learned that no matter how much I care,
some people just don't care back.
I've learned that either you control your attitude or it controls you.
I've learned that heroes are the people who do what has to be done when
it needs to be done, regardless of the consequences.
I've learned that there are people who love you dearly,
but just don't know how to show it.
I've learned that my best friend and I can do anything or nothing
and have the best time.
I've learned that sometimes the people you expect to kick you when
you're down may be the ones to help you back up.
I've learned that maturity has more to do with what types of experiences
you've had and what you've learned from them and less to do with how
many birthdays you've celebrated.
I've learned that if you don't want to forget something,
stick it in your underwear drawer.
I've learned that two people can look at the exact same thing
and see something totally different.
I've learned that you should never tell a child her dreams are unlikely or
outlandish. Few things are more humiliating,
and what a tragedy it would be if he or she believed it.
I've learned that no matter how bad your heart is broken
the world doesn't stop for your grief.
I've learned that no matter how many friends you have, if you are their
pillar, you will feel lonely and lost at the times you need them most.

The Sandpiper

Footprints in the Sand *by Mary Stevenson*

One night I dreamed I was walking along the beach with the Lord.
Many scenes from my life flashed across the sky.
In each scene I noticed footprints in the sand.
Sometimes there were two sets of footprints,
other times there were one set of footprints.

This bothered me because I noticed
that during the low periods of my life,
when I was suffering from
anguish, sorrow or defeat,
I could see only one set of footprints.

So I said to the Lord,
'You promised me Lord,
that if I followed you,
you would walk with me always.
But I have noticed that during
the most trying periods of my life
there has only been one
set of footprints in the sand.
Why, when I needed you most,
have you not been there for me?'

The Lord replied,
'The times when you have
seen only one set of footprints in the sand,
is when I carried you.'
There are some things you learn best in calm, and some in storm.

anon

• • •

Softly may Peace replace heartache,
And may warmest memories remain.

It's up to you

One song can spark a moment,
One flower can wake the dream,
One tree can start a forest,
One bird can herald spring

One smile begins a friendship,
One handclasp lifts a soul,
One star can guide a ship at sea,
One word can frame the goal.

One vote can change a nation,
One sunbeam lights a room,
One candle wipes out darkness,
One laugh will conquer gloom.

One step must start each journey,
One word must start each prayer,
One hope will raise our spirits,
One touch can show you care.

One voice can speak with wisdom
One heart can know what's true
One life can make the difference
You see, IT'S UP TO YOU! *anon.*

• • •

**Pooh and Piglet walked home thoughtfully together
in the golden evening, and for a long time they were silent.
'When you wake up in the morning, Pooh,' said Piglet at last,
'what's the first thing you say to yourself?'
'What's for breakfast?' said Pooh. 'What do you say, Piglet?'
'I say, I wonder what's going to happen exciting today?' said Piglet.
Pooh nodded thoughtfully.
'It's the same thing,' he said.** *A.A.Milne*

The Sandpiper

What will Matter *by Michael Josephson*

'Ready or not, some day it will all come to an end.
There will be no more sunrises, no minutes, hours or days.
All the things you collected, whether treasured or forgotten,
will pass to someone else.
Your wealth, fame and temporal power will shrivel to irrelevance.
It will not matter what you owned or what you were owed.
Your grudges, resentments, frustrations, and jealousies
will finally disappear.
So, too, your hopes, ambitions, plans, and to-do lists will expire.
The wins and losses that once seemed so important will fade away.
It won't matter where you came from,
or on what side of the tracks you lived, at the end.
It won't matter whether you were beautiful or brilliant.
Even your gender and skin colour will be irrelevant.
So what will matter? How will the value of your days be measured?
What will matter is not what you bought, but what you built;
not what you got, but what you gave.
What will matter is not your success, but your significance.
What will matter is not what you learned, but what you taught.
What will matter is every act of integrity, compassion,
courage or sacrifice that enriched, empowered
or encouraged others to emulate your example.
What will matter is not your competence, but your character.
What will matter is not how many people you knew,
but how many will feel a lasting loss when you're gone.
What will matter is not your memories,
but the memories that live in those who loved you.
What will matter is how long you will be remembered,
by whom and for what.
Living a life that matters doesn't happen by accident.
It's not a matter of circumstance but of choice.
Choose to live a life that matters.'

• • •

Live like a candle which burns itself
Yet gives light to others.
Look backwards with gratitude.
Upwards with confidence.
Forward with hope.
When you truly care for someone,
You don't look for faults.
You don't look for questions,
You don't look for answers.
Instead you fight the mistakes.
You accept the faults,
You overlook excuses and
You take each other to prayer.
A gentle reminder that the most
Precious thing in life cannot be
Built by man or bought by man
But can be able to see, to hear,
To touch, to taste, to feel and to love.

Written by an 18 year old rape victim, infected with HIV/AIDS

• • •

**'In one of the stars, I shall be living.
In one of them, I shall be laughing.
And so it will be as if all the stars were laughing
when you look at the sky at night.'**
from The Little Prince *by Antoine de Saint-Exupéry*

The Sandpiper

At Euston *by A.M. Harbord.*

Stranger with the pile of luggage proudly labelled for Portree,
How I wish this night of August I were you and you were me!
Think of all that lies before you when the train goes sliding forth.
And the lines athwart the sunset lead you swiftly to the North!
Think of breakfast at Kingussie, think of high Drumochter Pass.
Think of Highland breezes singing through the bracken and the grass.
Scabious blue and yellow daisy, tender fern beside the train,
Rowdy tummel falling, brawling, seen and lost and glimpsed again!
You will pass my golden roadway of the days of long ago:
Will you realise the magic of the names I used to know;
Clachnaharry, Achnashellash, Achnasheen and Duirinish?
Ev'ry moor alive with coveys, every pool aboil with fish;
Every well remembered vista more exciting by the mile.
Till the wheeling gulls are screaming round the engine at the Kyle
Think of cloud on Bheinn na Cailleach, jagged Cuillins soaring high
Scent of peat and all the glamour of the misty Isle of Skye!
Rods and gun case in the carriage, wise retriever in the van;
Go, and good luck travel with you! (Wish I'd half your luck, my man!)

• • •

Pack up my rod, the wind grows chill,
The hills are turning grey;
And I must up to catch a train
to take me far away,
Back into the world again,
But still, Thank God for such a day

anon

• • •

'They're funny things, Accidents. You never have them 'til you're having them.' *Eeyore by A.A. Milne*

Speak softly and carry a big stick

•••

It's Worth a Thought

This is a story about four people
named, everybody, somebody,
anybody and nobody.
There was an important job to be
done and everybody could have done it,
but nobody did it.
Somebody got angry about that
because it was everybody's job.
Everybody thought somebody could
do it, but nobody realised that
everybody wouldn't do it.
It ended up that everybody blamed
somebody when nobody did what
anybody could have done! *anon.*

The Sandpiper

An African Elegy *by Ben Okri*

We are the miracles that God made
To taste the bitter fruit of Time.
We are precious.
And one day our suffering
Will turn into the wonders of the earth.

There are things that burn me now
Which turn golden when I am happy.
Do you see the mystery of our pain?
That we bear the poverty
And are able to sing and dream sweet things.

And that we never curse the air when it is warm
Or the fruit when it tastes so good
Or the lights that bounce gently on the waters?
We bless the things even in our pain.
We bless them in silence.

That is why our music is so sweet.
It makes the air remember.
There are secret miracles at work
That only Time will bring forth.
I too have heard the dead singing.

And they tell me that
This life is good.
They tell me to live it gently
With fire, and always with hope.
There is wonder here

And there is surprise
In everything the unseen moves.
The ocean is full of songs.
The sky is not an enemy.
Destiny is our friend.

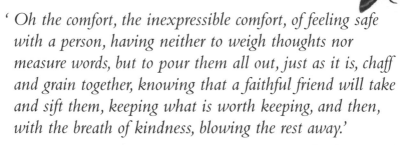

' *Oh the comfort, the inexpressible comfort, of feeling safe
with a person, having neither to weigh thoughts nor
measure words, but to pour them all out, just as it is, chaff
and grain together, knowing that a faithful friend will take
and sift them, keeping what is worth keeping, and then,
with the breath of kindness, blowing the rest away.*'

George Eliot (1819-1880)

• • •

When God had made the earth and sky
the flowers and the trees,
He then made all the animals
the fish, the birds and bees.
And when at last He'd finished
not one was quite the same.
He said, 'I'll walk this world of mine
and give each one a name.'
And so He travelled far and wide
and everywhere He went,
a little creature followed Him
until it's strength was spent.
When all were named upon the earth
and in the sky and sea,
the little creature said, 'Dear Lord,
there's not one left for me '
Kindly the Father said to him,
'I've left you to the end.
I've turned my own name back to front
and called you Dog, my friend.'

anon.

• • •

The Sandpiper

The Big Pack *by Patrick Chalmers (1872-1942)*

Where high the hills of heather
Heave to the skyline's rim–
Saddles and peaks together,
The great cloud shadows skim;
But faster than the wrack flies
Or e'er the shadow ran,
The pack, the wild grouse pack, flies;
Take toll of it who can!

I sing no heathbell's blushing,
No amethystine prime
With easy coveys flushing
In innocence sublime
Before the frozen setter,
But, in plain homespun, I
Would show you something better–
The best way birds can fly.

Proud August's past her blooming,
In gullies and in cuts
Down the big winds go booming
Upon some waiting butts
Where, talented and tenty,
sit men whose custom is
To pick up five and twenty
For thirty cartridges;

Afar a flag is flipping,
A little glag and gay;
A mile of moorland's slipping
Towards us, did you say?
A league of Perthshire heather
That moves and moves amain,
A hillside, hell for leather,
That 'comes to Dunsinane'?

Nay, here's no necromancy,
No mountains move on words,
That blur of blotted pansy
That's birds, that's birds, that's birds,
That's grouse, the gales for drover,
A headlong cloud go they,
They're up, they're on, they're over,
Take toll of 'em who may!

> **You'll find a partridge pleasant,**
> **The hedgerow russet-clad;**
> **And pleasant, too, the pheasant-**
> **A pheasant's not so bad,**
> **The guns, at Christmas, popping**
> **Around the manor house;**
> **But here's the stuff worth stopping,**
> **I've shown you driven grouse!**

• • •

Where there is love *by Helen Steiner Rice*

Where there is love the heart is light,
Where there is love the day is bright,
Where there is love there is song
To help when things are going wrong.

Where there is love there is a smile
To make all things seem more worthwhile.
Where there is love there is quiet peace
A tranquil place where turmoils cease.

Love changes darkness into light
And makes the heart take 'wingless flight'.
Oh blest are they who walk in love,
They also walk with God above.

The Sandpiper

There is hope...

Last year, an ex-serviceman proudly displaying his medals, travelled to London for the Remembrance Day service at the Cenotaph. He took at Black Taxi from the railway station to the Cenotaph and back. On both occasions when he asked the taxi driver how much he owed him for his journey, the response was the same. 'I owe you far more than you owe me' and bid him farewell. *anon.*

•••

She was one of those happily created beings who please without effort, make friends everywhere, and take life so gracefully and easily that less fortunate souls are tempted to believe that such are born under a lucky star.

from Little Women by Louise May Alcott (1832-1888)

Listen

When I ask you to listen to me and you start giving advice
you have not done what I asked.

When I ask you to listen to me and you begin to tell me why
I shouldn't feel that way you are trampling on my feelings.

When I ask you to listen to me and you feel you have to do something
to solve my problem you have failed me, strange as it may seem.

Listen! all I asked was that you listen-- not talk or do, just hear me.

When you do something for me that I can and need to do for myself,
you contribute to my fear and weakness.

But, when you accept as a simple fact that I do feel what I feel no matter
how irrational, then I can quit trying to convince you and can get about
the business of understanding what's behind this irrational feeling.
And when that's clear, the answers are obvious and I don't need advice.

Perhaps that's why prayer works, sometimes, for some people,
because God is mute, and he doesn't give advice or try to fix things.
'They' just listen and let you work it out for yourself.

So please listen and just hear me. And, if you want to talk,
wait a minute for your turn; and I'll listen to you! *anon.*

• • •

Some people come into our lives and quickly go.
Some people move our souls to dance.
They awaken us to new understanding
with the passing whisper of their wisdom.
Some people make the sky more beautiful to gaze upon.
They stay in our lives for a while,
leave footprints on our hearts,
and we are never ever the same.
Flavia Weedn

The Sandpiper

Warning – When I Am an Old Woman I Shall Wear Purple
by Jenny Joseph

When I am an old woman, I shall wear purple
with a red hat that doesn't go, and doesn't suit me.
And I shall spend my pension on brandy and summer gloves
and satin slippers, and say we've no money for butter.
I shall sit down on the pavement when I am tired
and gobble up samples in shops and press alarm bells
and run my stick along the public railings
and make up for the sobriety of my youth.
I shall go out in my slippers in the rain
and pick the flowers in other people's gardens
and learn to spit.
You can wear terrible shirts and grow more fat
and eat three pounds of sausages at a go
or only bread and pickles for a week
and hoard pens and pencils and beer mats and things in boxes.
But now we must have clothes that keep us dry
and pay our rent and not swear in the street
and set a good example for the children.
We will have friends to dinner and read the papers.
But maybe I ought to practise a little now?
So people who know me are not too shocked and surprised
When suddenly I am old, and start to wear purple.

• • •

Today a songbird sang –
Perched so high on yonder tree
Against a sky of silver grey
Full throated song to fill the air
And lift all care away –
I stayed to listen.

• • •

What are days for?
Days are
where we live.

Philip Larkin (1922-1985)

• • •

There is still a view – perhaps understandably – that illness is a negative life experience; one that disrupts normal lifestyle, daily routine, education and work – and one that can be associated with anxiety, fear and distress as well as the physical symptoms of the illness concerned.
We must try to offset these negative elements of illness with a positive approach in a positive environment, by putting some fun into worry, some colour into the dull, and some information into the unknown.
Professor George G. Youngson – Consultant Paediatric Surgeon, RACH

• • •

The glory of life is to love, not to be loved;
to give, not to get; to serve, not to be served;
to be a strong hand in the dark to another
in time of need.

Mahatma Gandhi

• • •

The Sandpiper

A Herbal Remedy for Life-ache *by Michael Leunig*

You suffer from life-ache
Your whole life is sore: it hurts when you move it.
Take one patch of grass, a mild day and two large green trees.
Lie on the grass beneath one tree and contemplate the other tree.
Nap from time to time or gaze occasionally at the grass.
Pain will subside.
Life-ache cannot be cured.
But you can learn to manage the symptoms.

• • •

The kiss of the sun for pardon,
The song of the birds for mirth.
One is nearer to God's heart in the garden
Than anywhere else on earth.

Dorothy Gurney (1858 - 1952)

• • •

66 Through the fields of happiness and of unequalled beauty
runs the path of life, only stopping now and then
at some burnt piece of land or dead tree,
showing that here, sadness has stretched her fingers
and touched the unhappy few.

To survive, one must have happiness.
One encouraging word, a sunshine smile
and the freedom that goes with life is all yours. 99
anon.

When the tide
of life turns
against you
and the current
upsets your boat,
Don't waste
your tears
on what might
have been,
Just lie on your
back and float.

The Sandpiper

In Memoriam *from Thinning Grapes by Mary Sheepshanks*

You do not need memorials of brass
on cold church walls;
your name is written on the wind-streaked sky
over the open moors
where red-grouse call.

> **I do not want your epitaph on stone**
> **carved around a tomb:**
> **your story can be read in flowers and shrubs**
> **and those rare trees you planted**
> **round our home.**

I shall not hoard mementoes in a box
with plaque inlaid:
your spirit will live on while I can keep
green memories of the garden
that you made.

• • •

When he dies,
then I hope I may follow,
and to where the racehorses go.
I don't want no harping
nor singing –
Such things with my style
don't agree,
Where the hoofs of the horses
are ringing
There's music sufficient for me'

The Call *by Thomas Osbert Mordaunt (1730-1809)*

Sound, sound the clarion, fill the fife!
Throughout the sensual world proclaim,
One crowded hour of glorious life
Is worth an age without a name.

•••

Time and tide

wait for no man

•••

**Work like you don't need
the money
Love like you've never been hurt
Dance like nobody's watching
Sing like nobody's listening
Live like its Heaven on Earth**

•••

Postscript

'I like spring, but it is too young.
I like summer, but it is too proud.
So I like best of all autumn,
because its leaves are a little yellow,
its tone mellower,
its colours richer and it is tinged a little with sorrow...
Its golden richness speaks not of the innocence of spring,
nor of the power of summer,
but of the mellowness and kindly wisdom of approaching age.
It knows the limitations of life and is content.'
Lin Yutang (1895-1976)

For more than 30 years I have worked as a rural general practitioner and a palliative care physician. I have had the privilege of sharing both happy and sad times with many patients and families. I have witnessed loss and suffering in all their guises – sometimes predictable and inevitable, sometimes sudden and tragic. The questions 'Why me?', 'Why him or her?, 'Why now?', 'Why this?' remain, as always, unanswered.

We are however remarkable beings. I have come to appreciate that we face adversity and loss in ways which are unique to each individual. The support and love of family, friends and for some, pets, are invaluable. Spiritual comfort may be derived not only from faith but from music, the written word, memories which can never be eroded and special places (for me, a particular spot in the wilds of Wester Ross will always be my spiritual haven).

We will always face adversity, illness, suffering and loss in our own way but the contents of this book illustrate the power of words and the solace that can be obtained both by writing them and reading them.

Dr David Carroll
Roxburghe House, Aberdeen

Index of first lines

**...and you'll remember me
when the west wind moves
Upon the fields of barley.**

from Fields of Gold by Sting -1993

*Contributed by Claire Maitland in memory
of her father John Drysdale (1929 -2008)
to whom this book is also dedicated*

The **S**wallow, The **O**wl & The **S**andpiper

Acknowledgements

I would like to thank the following: Firstly my husband **Robin**, and children **Harry, Cara, Anna**, and **Jack** for encouraging me all the way and for sharing Sunday lunches with my 'office' space at one end of the kitchen table. I have thoroughly enjoyed our lively debates whilst trying to catagorise the prose and poetry between The Courage of The Swallow, The Wisdom of the Owl, and The Spirit of The Sandpiper; Everyone who took the time to send me their own personal choice of words and the authors, without whom this book simply wouldn't have happened; **Rodger McPhail** for his generous donation of artwork; **Robert Harrison** of Fettes College, Edinburgh, for taking time to proof read the book; **Gavin Hastings**, Patron of The Sandpiper Trust, for his great support and friendship; **Dr Colville Laird** and **Dr Ewen McLeod** of BASICS-Scotland for their invaluable guidance as medical directors to the charity; **Strutt and Parker** for their continuing support; The authors **Mary Sheepshanks** and **Michael J Rosen** for their words of encouragement; The Sandpiper Elves **Joanna Aberdeen**, **Virginia Fyffe**, **Miranda McHardy** and **Kate Robertson**; **Fiona Hill**, of Finks Publishing, for her patience in putting this all together. **And finally...** My sister **Penny** and brother-in-law **Alistair Dickson** for accompanying me on this Sandpiper Journey. My admiration for them and the way that they have coped following the loss of their son Sandy knows no bounds. I have tried to meet copyright requirements and trace authors but in some cases this has proved impossible for which I apologise.

Claire Maitland – The Sandpiper Trust